Reading & Writing
Easter Island

Australia • Brazil • Mexico • Singapore • United Kingdom • United States

National Geographic Learning,
a Cengage Company

Reading & Writing, Easter Island

Lauri Blass, Mari Vargo, Keith S. Folse, April Muchmore-Vokoun, Elena Vestri, Tison Pugh

Publisher: Sherrise Roehr

Executive Editor: Laura LeDréan

Managing Editor: Jennifer Monaghan

Digital Implementation Manager, Irene Boixareu

Senior Media Researcher: Leila Hishmeh

Director of Global Marketing: Ian Martin

Regional Sales and National Account Manager: Andrew O'Shea

Content Project Manager: Ruth Moore

Senior Designer: Lisa Trager

Manufacturing Planner: Mary Beth Hennebury

Composition: Lumina Datamatics

Student Edition: Reading & Writing, Easter Island
ISBN-13: 978-0-357-13836-6

National Geographic Learning
20 Channel Center Street
Boston, MA 02210
USA

Locate your local office at **international.cengage.com/region**

Visit National Geographic Learning online at **ELTNGL.com**
Visit our corporate website at **www.cengage.com**

Printed in China
Print Number: 02 Print Year: 2019

PHOTO CREDITS

1 Nick Kaloterakis/National Geographic Creative, **5** Brendan McDermid/Reuters, **11** © Day's Edge Productions, **14** Danita Delimont/Alamy Stock Photo, **16** Chris Ratcliffe/Bloomberg via Getty Images, **24-25** © Allen Yang/Flickr/Getty Images, **26** © Peter Essick/National Geographic Image Collection, **31** © KEENPRESS/National Geographic Creative, **40** © Jay Fleming/Corbis, **45:** © Mark Hall/Shutterstock.com, **48** © Danil Melekhin/Getty Images, **57** Michael Nichols/National Geographic Creative, **58** Janette Hill/National Geographic Creative, **59** (cr) (bl) (tl) Joel Sartore/National Geographic Creative, **60** James R.D. Scott/Getty Images, **62** Steve Winter/National Geographic Creative, **64** Steve Winter/National Geographic Creative, **66** (b) Steve Winter/National Geographic Creative, (cr) Evan Agostini/Getty Images, **70** Konrad Wothe/Minden Pictures, **72** Joel Sartore/National Geographic Creative, **74** Dmitrij Skorobogatov/Shutterstock, **76** National Geographic Creative, **79** Joel Sartore/National Geographic Creative, **80-81** Juan Velasco/National Geographic Creative, **83** Ralf Dujmovits/National Geographic Creative, **85** Gerlinde Kaltenbrunner/National Geographic Creative, **89** David Doubilet/National Geographic Creative, **92** Arun Sankar/Getty Images, **93** Alison Wright/National Geographic Creative, **94** Alison Wright/National Geographic Creative

Scope and Sequence

Unit Title and Theme	Reading Texts and Video	ACADEMIC SKILLS Reading
1 **GLOBAL CHALLENGES** *page 1* ACADEMIC TRACK: Environmental Science	**Reading 1** A Need for Change **VIDEO** The Snow Guardian **Reading 2** Eight Steps to a Sustainable Future	**Focus** Understanding Appositives Predicting, Understanding Main Ideas, Understanding Details, Interpreting Visual Information, Understanding Problems and Solutions, Inferring Meaning

Unit Title and Theme	Writing	Grammar for Writing
2 **ARGUMENT ESSAYS** *page 24*	What Is an Argument Essay? How Is an Argument Essay Organized? Great Topics for Argument Essays Strong Thesis Statements for Argument Essays Strong Counterargument and Refutation Statements for Argument Essays Transitions and Connectors in Argument Essays	Modals *-ly* Adverbs of Degree

Unit Title and Theme	Reading Texts and Video	ACADEMIC SKILLS Reading
3 **ON THE EDGE** *page 57* ACADEMIC TRACK: Life Science/Conservation	**Reading** A Cry for the Tiger by Caroline Alexander (explanatory/persuasive report) **VIDEO** Tigers in the Snow	**Focus** Understanding Appositives Understanding Main Ideas and Details, Identifying Problems, Reasons and Solutions

Unit Title and Theme	Reading Texts and Video	ACADEMIC SKILLS Reading
4 **SURVIVAL INSTINCT** *page 79* ACADEMIC TRACK: Psychology	**Reading 1** Deadly Summit **VIDEO** Survival Lessons **Reading 2** Breath of Life	**Focus** Identifying Adverbial Phrases Skimming, Summarizing, Understanding Main Ideas, Sequencing, Inferring Meaning, Predicting, Understanding Details

Critical Thinking	Writing	Vocabulary Extension
Focus Inferring Attitude Evaluating	**Skill Focus** Writing an Opinion Essay **Language for Writing** Using Adjective Clauses **Writing Goal** Revise parts of an opinion essay	**Word Partners** Expressions with *cut*

Building Better Vocabulary	Original Student Writing
Practicing Three Kinds of Vocabulary from Context: Synonyms, Antonyms, and Collocations	**Original Student Writing** Write an argument essay. **Photo Topic** Write about whether older people should have a driver's license. **Timed Writing Topic** Write about whether people should eat a vegetarian diet.

Critical Thinking	Writing	Vocabulary Extension
Focus Analyzing Text Organization Personalizing, Making Inferences, Synthesizing, Guessing Meaning from Context	**Skill Focus** Reviewing the thesis statement **Language for Writing** Using appositives **Writing Goal** Revise parts of an opinion essay	**Word Partners** Adjective/verb + *priority*

Critical Thinking		Vocabulary Extension
Focus Interpreting Figurative Language Reflecting, Applying, Synthesizing		**Word Forms** Adjectives ending in *-ed* and *-ing*

GLOBAL CHALLENGES 1

If all the ice in the world melted, coastal cities such as New York would be mostly underwater.

ACADEMIC SKILLS

READING Understanding appositives
WRITING Writing an opinion essay
GRAMMAR Using adjective clauses
CRITICAL THINKING Inferring attitude

THINK AND DISCUSS

1 What are some potential effects of rising sea levels?
2 Why do you think sea levels are rising?

EXPLORE THE THEME

A Look at the information on these pages and answer the questions.

1. What does the size of each area on the map represent? What do the different colors represent?
2. What do you think this map will look like 30 years from now?

B Match the words and phrases in blue to their definitions.

________________ (adv) at this moment

________________ (adj) connected to

________________ (adv) concerning the whole planet

OUR HUMAN IMPACT

What impact do we have on Earth's resources? One way to measure this is to look at Gross Domestic Product (GDP)—the amount of goods and services produced in one year. GDP numbers are **related to** consumption—the using up of resources. A high GDP per capita equates with a higher standard of living, which in turn is likely to mean a higher rate of natural resource consumption.

This map shows GDP levels **worldwide**. Each area is sized according to its GDP, rather than to its physical area. The colors indicate the GDP per person in each area. As the map shows, wealthier regions such as North America **currently** have the highest GDP levels—and therefore the greatest environmental impact—but emerging economies such as China and India are catching up fast.

Reading 1

PREPARING TO READ

BUILDING VOCABULARY

A The words and phrases in blue below are used in Reading 1. Read the sentences. Then match the correct form of each word or phrase to its definition.

Many scientists believe that climate change is a **crucial** global issue today.

Cars and factories **generate** greenhouse gases, which contribute to global warming.

Warming temperatures are causing Arctic sea ice to **shrink** rapidly. Eventually, all the sea ice may **vanish** completely.

Because of the **exceptional** increase in global temperatures, sixteen of the warmest years ever recorded have occurred since 2000.

Scientists are identifying **practical** ways that individuals and countries can help solve this problem, such as by **focusing on** alternative energy sources.

1. ____________ (v) to disappear
2. ____________ (adj) extremely important
3. ____________ (adj) likely to be effective or useful
4. ____________ (v) to produce or create
5. ____________ (adj) much greater than usual
6. ____________ (v) to pay attention to
7. ____________ (v) to get smaller

USING VOCABULARY

B Discuss these questions with a partner.

1. What is a **crucial** problem in your town or city right now?
2. What are some **practical** ways that you can deal with it?

BRAINSTORMING

C Note your answers to these questions. Then discuss with a partner.

1. What do you think is the most important environmental issue that we face today?

____

2. What are two ways to educate people about this environmental issue?

____

PREDICTING

D Read the first paragraph and the three interview questions in the reading passage. What topics do you think DiCaprio will talk about? Discuss with a partner. Then check your ideas as you read.

A NEED FOR CHANGE

Track 1

A Oscar-winning actor Leonardo DiCaprio likes to say that he makes his living in made-up worlds. Now DiCaprio, a UN Messenger of Peace, has produced a documentary about a very real concern: climate change. He shot *Before the Flood* all over the world—this time playing himself.

B DiCaprio became a climate activist after a 1998 meeting with former U.S. Vice President Al Gore, an early advocate for climate change education. The meeting inspired him to launch the Leonardo DiCaprio Foundation. The foundation has awarded over 60 million dollars to individuals and organizations that are working to protect wildlife, indigenous communities, and the planet.

C In the documentary *Before the Flood*, DiCaprio investigates the impact of climate change around the globe. In his introductory speech at the film's London premiere, DiCaprio said, "We wanted to make a film that gave people a sense of urgency, [and] that made them understand what particular things are going to solve the problem." In late 2016, *National Geographic* interviewed DiCaprio about *Before the Flood*. This interview was edited for length and clarity.

Q: Who do you hope to reach with the film?

D **DiCaprio:** We all have a role to play in saving our planet. This film is meant to educate everyone, from global leaders to everyday citizens, on the threat of climate change. There are practical steps we all must take—today—to hasten[1] the adoption of renewable and clean-energy technologies across the planet. For the film we interviewed inspiring figures, from Pope Francis and President Obama, who both have the ability to galvanize[2] millions of people, to activists like Sunita Narain, a tremendous voice in India who's calling for her country to be part of a global solution.

[1] To **hasten** means to speed something up.
[2] If you **galvanize** people, you motivate them to take action.

> "Climate change is real, it is happening right now, it is the most urgent threat facing our entire species."

Q: How can an issue like climate change attract more sustained attention?

E

DiCaprio: There is no issue this important—because the future of the planet is at stake.[3] We have no planet B. The energy we **focus on** solving climate change and the pressure we place on global leaders to lead on the question will help create a sustainable and livable environment for the long term.

Q: You traveled around the world for this film. What message do people have for Americans?

F

DiCaprio: We need to vote for leaders who understand the serious issues impacting our climate—and for leaders who believe in the undeniable truth of science. No nation or society is immune[4] to the symptoms of climate change. America is in many places already feeling the impacts of it: droughts in California, rising seas in Miami, more extreme storms in the Gulf of Mexico. We can still prevent these crises from becoming a widespread challenge in the future of our country. We have an opportunity to lead the world on one of the most **crucial** issues of all time.

[3] If something is **at stake**, it's at risk; it could be lost or be in danger.

[4] If a person or a thing is **immune**, it will not be affected by another person or thing.

SEVEN FACTS ABOUT CLIMATE CHANGE

1. The world is warming.

G

Earth's temperature goes up and down from year to year—but over the past half-century, it has gone up a lot (Fig. 1). The trend **currently** looks set to continue: the heat in 2016 broke the historic record set in 2015, which broke the one from 2014.

2. It's because of us.

H

Carbon dioxide warms the planet, and we've increased the amount in the air by nearly half, mostly since the 1960s (Fig. 2). Events such as El Niño—a climate cycle in the Pacific Ocean—also affect global temperatures. But no natural cause explains the half-century warming trend.

3. We're sure.

I

More than 9 out of 10 climate scientists agree: Carbon emissions cause global warming. A 2013 review

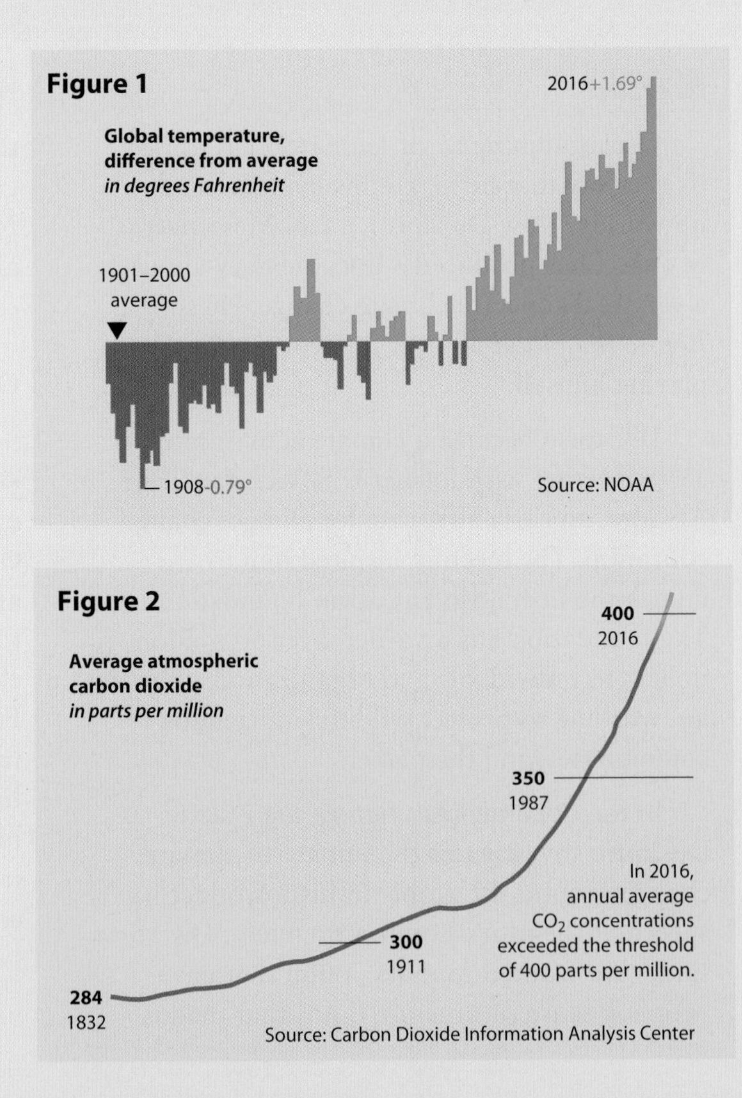

of more than 4,000 research papers found that 97 percent said humans cause global warming.

4. Ice is melting fast.

The Arctic has warmed more than the rest of the planet, and its sea ice is **shrinking** (Fig. 3). The ice loss speeds up global warming because more sunlight is absorbed by dark oceans instead of being reflected into space by the ice. Warming temperatures also mean the retreat of mountain glaciers **worldwide**. Together, these factors contribute to rising sea levels, which could rise by three feet by 2100—or maybe more.

5. Weather is getting intense.

Globally, the number of disasters **related to** climate has more than tripled since 1980 (Fig. 4). The extraordinary heat wave that killed some 70,000 people in Europe in 2003 should have been a once-in-500-years event; at the current level of global warming, it has become a once-in-40-years event. If global warming continues unchecked, by the end of this century, regions such as the Arabian Gulf may see days that are so hot that it will be unsafe to go outside.

6. Wildlife is already hurting.

Animals and plants are already **vanishing** from parts of their range that are now too hot. Extinctions come next. A 2016 study showed that of 976 species surveyed, 47 percent had vanished from areas on the warm edge of their range. The **exceptional** ocean warmth of the past few years has also devastated many of the world's coral reefs. Some species will adapt to the changing climate—but how many, and for how long?

7. We can do something about it.

The use of renewables—such as solar and wind energy—is projected to triple 1990 levels by 2040. Meanwhile, costs are falling, and are expected to decrease significantly from 2010

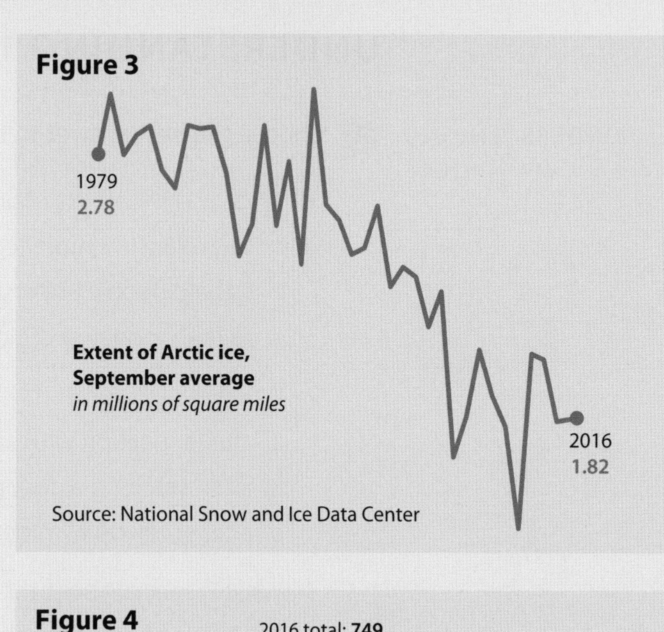

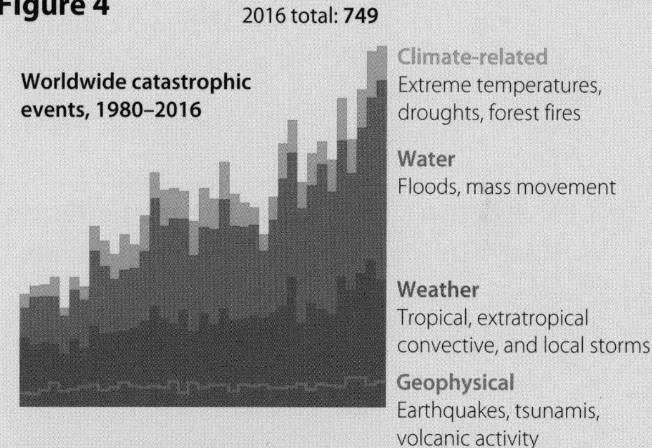

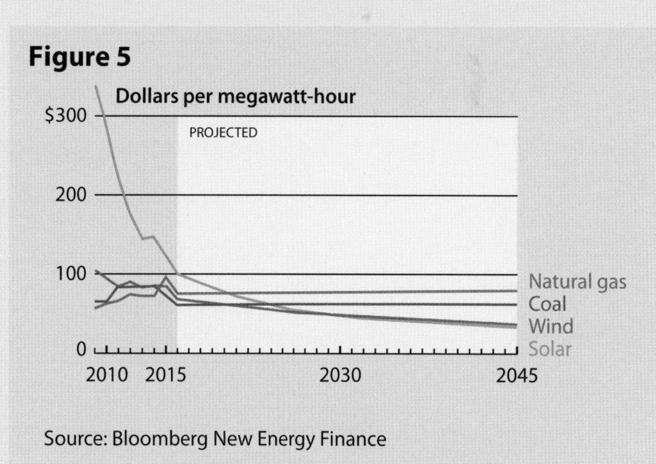

levels (Fig. 5). By 2040, the cost of wind power is estimated to decrease by over 50 percent, and solar power prices may decrease by 500 percent. Carbon-free renewable sources may soon be cheaper than the fossil fuels that **generate** carbon, providing hope for a more sustainable future.

UNDERSTANDING THE READING

UNDERSTANDING MAIN IDEAS

A **Choose the best answer to the questions about the interview.**

1. What was DiCaprio's main purpose for making *Before the Flood*?
   a. to explain in simple terms how the polar ice caps are melting
   b. to help people understand and want to solve the problem of climate change
   c. to raise money and global awareness for the Leonardo DiCaprio Foundation
2. When did DiCaprio first become interested in the issue of climate change?
   a. after a meeting with an influential politician
   b. after watching a documentary about the issue
   c. after speaking with people in areas affected by rising seas
3. What is special about the people that DiCaprio interviewed?
   a. They were the first scientists to identify the issue of global warming.
   b. They have all invented technologies for dealing with rising sea levels.
   c. They are individuals who can motivate people to fight climate change.

UNDERSTANDING MAIN IDEAS

B **Complete the sentences about the main ideas of the section "Seven Facts about Climate Change." Write no more than two words in each space.**

1. The Earth's temperature is increasing, especially in the last ________________.
2. Climate change is mostly caused by ________________ activities, not ________________ events.
3. Most ________________ agree that climate change is caused by ________________ emissions.
4. Loss of sea ice in the Arctic is ________________ global warming.
5. Global warming is causing extreme ________________ events to happen more ________________.
6. Wildlife species are ________________ due to warming temperatures.
7. There are solutions to the problem. Renewable energy is likely to become ________________ than fossil fuels in the future.

UNDERSTANDING DETAILS

C **Read the statements (1–7). For each statement, circle T for true, F for false, or NG if the information is not given.**

1. The Earth's temperature in 2016 was hotter than in 2014. **T F NG**
2. Atmospheric carbon dioxide levels have doubled since the 1990s. **T F NG**
3. Factory emissions are the biggest contributor to global warming. **T F NG**
4. Sea levels could rise three feet by 2100. **T F NG**

5. Major heat waves are becoming more common in the United States. **T** **F** **NG**
6. Nearly half of species in a 2016 study had disappeared from warmer edges of their range. **T** **F** **NG**
7. Solar power is expected to be 50% cheaper by 2040. **T** **F** **NG**

D **Match the graphs from the reading passage (Figures 1–5) with the descriptions (a–g). Two descriptions are extra.**

INTERPRETING VISUAL INFORMATION

_____ a. decrease in the amount of ice in the Arctic in the last few decades

_____ b. comparison of future costs of energy sources

_____ c. main causes of global temperature changes

_____ d. rise in carbon dioxide in the atmosphere in the last two centuries

_____ e. increase in serious events caused by changing climates

_____ f. changes in different types of energy usage over time

_____ g. changes in global temperatures over 115 years

CRITICAL THINKING To **infer** a person's **attitude**, look for words and expressions that show what they think about a topic, such as *important, awful, great, terrible, hope, hopeless,* etc. Also, look for modals such as *may, might, should, can, must, have to,* or *need to.* These can show attitudes such as urgency, optimism, or seriousness.

E **Which of the following (a–c) best describes DiCaprio's attitude toward the problem? Underline examples in the passage that support your answer.**

CRITICAL THINKING: INFERRING ATTITUDE

a. He believes that we are in an extremely dangerous situation and is frustrated that we have left it too late.
b. It is a very urgent problem, but if enough people work together, he is optimistic that a solution is possible.
c. He believes that changes in government policies are the best way to handle this problem.

F **DiCaprio says that climate change is "the most urgent threat facing our entire species." Do you agree with his view? Why or why not? Note your ideas and discuss with a partner.**

CRITICAL THINKING: EVALUATING

I **agree** / **disagree** with DiCaprio's view because ______________________________

____

____.

DEVELOPING READING SKILLS

READING SKILL Understanding Appositives

Look at the sentence below.

NOUN APPOSITIVE

*Now DiCaprio, **a UN Messenger of Peace,** has produced a documentary.*

The **appositive** "a UN Messenger of Peace" describes the noun "DiCaprio." It gives more information about the noun that it is describing.

Appositives take the form of a noun or a noun phrase. They explain, define, or give more information about another noun or noun phrase that is close to them. Appositives can come before or after the noun they describe.

Writers can use commas, dashes, parentheses, or colons to separate appositives from the nouns or noun phrases that they describe.

NOUN PHRASE APPOSITIVE

*The documentary is about a very real concern: **climate change**.*

UNDERSTANDING APPOSITIVES

A **Read each sentence from the passage. Underline the appositive and circle the noun or noun phrase that it refers to.**

1. Oscar-winning actor Leonardo DiCaprio likes to say that he makes his living in made-up worlds.
2. DiCaprio became a climate activist after a 1998 meeting with former U.S. Vice President Al Gore, ...
3. For the film we interviewed inspiring figures ... like Sunita Narain, a tremendous voice in India who's calling for her country to be part of a global solution.
4. Events such as El Niño—a climate cycle in the Pacific Ocean—also affect global temperatures.

UNDERSTANDING APPOSITIVES

B **Match each appositive (a–d) to the noun or noun phrase it refers to.**

a. an American director and producer

b. one of the oldest entertainment awards ceremonies in the world

c. ones that are fitted with filters

d. located on the East Coast of the United States

1. The Oscars, ____, takes place every year.
2. *Jurassic Park* is one of the most famous movies that Steven Spielberg, ____, is known for.
3. New York University, ____, has produced famous filmmakers such as Martin Scorsese and Ang Lee.
4. People have to put on special glasses—____—in order to view a movie in 3-D.

APPLYING

C **Scan for and write two examples of appositives in the Explore the Theme section. Share your answers with a partner.**

1. ____________________

2. ____________________

Video

billy barr has lived alone in Gothic, Colorado, for more than 40 years.

THE SNOW GUARDIAN

BEFORE VIEWING

A Read the caption and title of the video. What do you think the video is about? PREDICTING

B Read the information about a town in Colorado and answer the questions. LEARNING ABOUT THE TOPIC

Gothic, Colorado, used to be a ghost town—a once-successful town that was later abandoned. For almost twenty years in the late 19th century, Gothic had a silver mine and almost 1,000 people lived and worked there. By the end of the 19th century, the silver was gone, and almost everyone had left.

In 1928, a scientist bought the town and started a research facility called Rocky Mountain Biological Laboratory. Today, about 160 scientists, professors, and students live and work in Gothic during the summers, studying local animals and climate change. One resident, billy barr (who doesn't capitalize his name), has lived in Gothic since 1972 and works as an accountant for the lab.

1. Why did most people leave Gothic?

 ____

2. What brought people back to Gothic?

 ____

3. Why do you think Gothic is a suitable place for doing scientific research?

 ____

 ____

VOCABULARY IN CONTEXT

C The words in **bold** below are used in the video. Read the sentences. Then match each word to its definition.

> Scientists keep **meticulous** records of their experiments. If they don't take careful and accurate notes, other people won't be able to duplicate their experiments.
>
> Children often have a great sense of **curiosity** and ask many questions about how things work.
>
> Some people think we might be able to **reverse** climate change if we reduce the amount of greenhouse gas emissions into the air.

1. ________________ (n) a feeling of wanting to know or learn about things
2. ________________ (adj) extremely thorough and with a lot of care for details
3. ________________ (v) to change something to be the opposite of what it is

WHILE VIEWING

UNDERSTANDING MAIN IDEAS

A ▶ Watch the video. Circle the correct options to answer the questions.

1. Why did billy barr first start recording data on snow?
   a. He was bored and wanted something to do.
   b. He was a researcher for a university.
   c. He wanted to gather evidence of climate change.
2. Which is the most suitable description of barr's attitude toward the problem?
   a. He feels confident that we can still reverse the situation if we put in more effort.
   b. He is seeing some signs of improvement after years of studying the snow.
   c. He thinks the problem is serious and is not sure how the situation can be fixed.

UNDERSTANDING DETAILS

B ▶ Watch the video again. Complete the sentences about the trends that barr has observed.

1. The permanent ________________ comes later than it used to.
2. The ground becomes ________________ sooner than it used to.
3. There are usually ________________ record high temperatures in a typical winter, but barr once recorded ________________.
4. Snow is melting faster than before because of more ________________ covering the snow.

AFTER VIEWING

REACTING TO THE VIDEO

A Would you like to conduct scientific research in a place like Gothic, Colorado? What are some of the location's advantages or disadvantages? Discuss with a partner.

CRITICAL THINKING: EVALUATING

B Work with a partner. What might be some limitations to billy barr's data? Do you think his data is a reliable indicator of climate change? Why or why not?

Reading 2

PREPARING TO READ

A The words and phrases in **blue** below are used in Reading 2. Read the sentences. Then circle the correct options to complete the definitions.

BUILDING VOCABULARY

By recycling paper and plastic, we can **cut down on** the amount of garbage we produce.

Car engines **emit** carbon dioxide (CO_2), which is a **major** contributor to global warming. Some countries have created laws to **regulate** the emissions from vehicles on the road.

The world's oil supplies are **limited**, and with current rates of usage, we are in danger of **exhausting** them. Some scientists think we will **consume** all of the world's oil supplies by 2070.

Solar panels **convert** the heat of the sun into energy that can be used to power homes.

Installing solar panels can help homeowners get a **reduction** in their electricity bills. More homeowners now **invest** in solar panels and put them on their roofs.

1. To *regulate* something means to **control** / **advertise** something.
2. When a factory *emits* a gas, it **releases** / **contains** it.
3. When you *convert* something, you **increase** / **change** it.
4. If you *exhaust* something, you **use it often** / **use it up completely**.
5. If you *consume* something, such as a resource, you **use it up** / **give it away**.
6. A *major* factor is something that plays **a specific** / **an important** role.
7. A *reduction* is **an increase** / **a decrease** in size, amount, or degree.
8. If you *cut down on* something, you **use less of it** / **divide it up**.
9. If something is *limited* in quantity, there is **a lot** / **not a lot** of it.
10. If you *invest* in something, such as a business, you **get money from** / **put money into** it.

B Work with a partner. What do you **consume** a lot of? What would you like to **cut down on**?

USING VOCABULARY

C Reading 2 is about eight ways we can create a sustainable future. What steps do you think people can take to achieve this? Discuss with a partner. Then check your ideas as you read.

PREDICTING

Salish Kootenai Dam in Montana, U.S.A., generates enough electricity to power more than 100,000 homes.

EIGHT STEPS TO A SUSTAINABLE FUTURE

Track 2

A We humans have unlimited appetites,[1] but we live on a planet with **limited** resources. We already use more of Earth's renewable resources—such as forests, clean air, and fresh water—than nature can restore each year. And when the rate of consumption of a resource is greater than the rate at which it is replaced, the resource may become exhausted.

B Today, Earth's population stands at around seven billion, and it is still growing fast. By 2050, there may be nine billion people living on the planet. As a result, the imbalance between what nature replaces and what humans **consume** will probably continue to grow. So how will so many more people live on Earth without **exhausting** the planet?

C The key is sustainability—finding new and efficient ways of conserving resources so that we do not use them all up. Here are eight steps to sustainability from around the world.

1. SUSTAINABLE COMMUNITIES

D Sustainable cities and towns encourage residents to reduce their impact on both the local and global environments. Residents in Mbam, Senegal, for example, use solar ovens to cook food. By using energy from the sun instead of burning wood, people are saving trees for future generations. Communities in other places are using improved public transportation systems so that people do not use cars as much. In Curitiba, Brazil, city buses are frequent, convenient, and efficient, so 70 percent of the city's commuters use them. As a result, the city has little traffic congestion[2] and cleaner air.

2. SAFER PRODUCTION

E As meat consumption grows, the environmental and health effects of producing meat grow as well. For example, the animal waste that results from raising animals for food can cause water pollution. In addition, farms that are close to

[1] People's **appetites** for things are their strong desires for them.

[2] **Traffic congestion** occurs when there are a lot of vehicles on the road, making movement slower.

city centers can increase the risk of dangerous diseases—such as avian flu[3]—spreading. Some governments are using tax breaks to solve this problem. The government of Thailand placed a high tax on poultry farms that were within 62 miles (100 kilometers) of its capital city, Bangkok. As a result, many poultry producers moved away from the city center.

3. CLEANER POWER

Sun and wind power are two energy sources that are renewable and that do not pollute the environment. Harvesting solar energy is an increasing trend. One method is via the use of photovoltaic cells (PVs), cells

F that **convert** solar energy to electricity. By 2017, PVs produced more than 300 gigawatts[4] of power worldwide. **Major** solar energy producers include Germany, China, and the United States. Global wind power production grew by about 2,000 percent in the 15 years between 2001 and 2016, and it is still growing. As of 2016, China was the leader in wind power, producing over 168,000 megawatts of wind energy. The United States and Germany are also major wind power producers.

4. SOCIAL INVESTMENT

People who practice socially responsible investing (SRI) buy shares in companies that focus on practices that are good for the planet, like **cutting down on** landfill[5] waste and creating alternative energy. While SRI activity is most

G common in Europe and the United States, it is growing quickly in Canada and Australia, too. There is also an increasing number of people in South Korea, Brazil, Malaysia, and South Africa who are practicing SRI.

5. GREENER LIGHTBULBS

H The popularity of LED (light emitting diode) lightbulbs has been growing quickly since 2001.

[3] **Avian flu,** or **bird flu,** is a virus transmitted from birds to humans.
[4] A watt is a unit of measurement of electrical power. A **gigawatt** is one billion watts.

[5] A **landfill** is an area where garbage is buried in the ground.

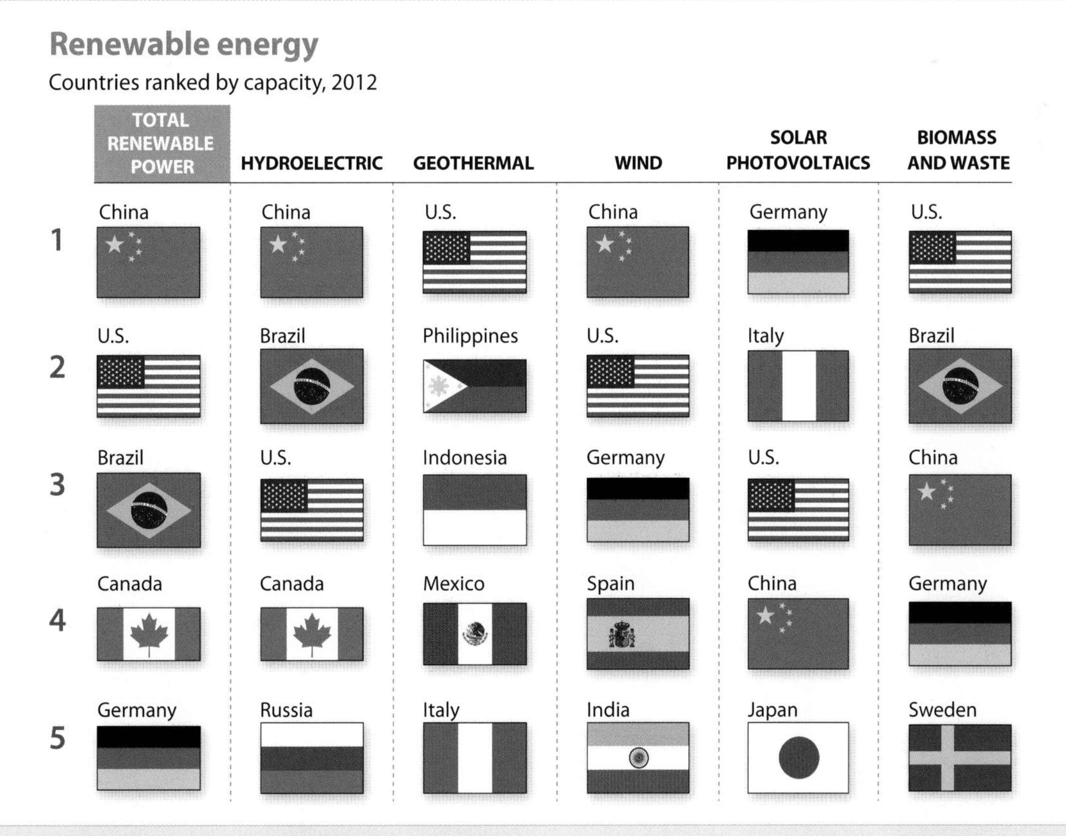

Renewable energy
Countries ranked by capacity, 2012

	TOTAL RENEWABLE POWER	HYDROELECTRIC	GEOTHERMAL	WIND	SOLAR PHOTOVOLTAICS	BIOMASS AND WASTE
1	China	China	U.S.	China	Germany	U.S.
2	U.S.	Brazil	Philippines	U.S.	Italy	Brazil
3	Brazil	U.S.	Indonesia	Germany	U.S.	China
4	Canada	Canada	Mexico	Spain	China	Germany
5	Germany	Russia	Italy	India	Japan	Sweden

Note: hydroelectric: generating power through movement of water
geothermal: heat energy from deep within Earth

This is because they use 75 percent less energy than traditional lightbulbs and last 25 times longer. Currently, about 16 percent of all lightbulbs sold are LEDs. However, by the year 2022, LEDs will make up 50 percent of the global market share.

6. CERTIFIED FORESTS

Logging—the cutting down of trees—has several negative effects on the environment. For example, it can lead to water pollution and destroy animal habitats. In an effort to cut down on these effects, several countries are creating certified forests. When a forest is certified, I the logging is **regulated** and done in a sustainable way. In West Virginia (U.S.A.), for example, loggers must get special training. Roughly ten percent of the world's forests are certified. Canada has the largest areas, with about 410 million acres (166 million hectares) of certified forests.

7. GREEN EMPLOYMENT

About 10 million people around the world work in the renewable energy industry; this number has grown by almost 7 million in ten years. Sixty-two percent of these jobs are in Asia, J but green jobs are growing in other countries, too. Denmark, for example, produces a large number of the world's wind turbines,[6] and the Kenyan government has **invested** more than one billion dollars jointly with private companies to build solar power plants across the country.

8. LOWER EMISSIONS

Carbon emissions continue to contribute to climate change. Since 1970, emissions from fossil fuels—such as coal, oil, and natural gas—have increased about 200 percent. However, some K countries are committed to reversing this trend. Brazil, for example, has promised to **emit** 37 percent less CO_2 by 2025, compared to 2005 levels. In addition, India and Nigeria are planning major **reductions** by 2030.

[6] **Wind turbines** are machines that produce electricity, using large blades that are turned by the wind.

A worker testing one of the world's largest wind turbines in Denmark

UNDERSTANDING THE READING

A Complete the main ideas of the reading passage using the words below. One word can be used more than once.

UNDERSTANDING MAIN IDEAS

regulating	**investing**	**making**	**reducing**	**motivating**	**using**	**increasing**

Eight steps to sustainability:

1. ________________ people to lower their impact on the environment and their cities
2. ________________ the production of livestock safer
3. ________________ more renewable energy sources
4. ________________ in companies that try to protect the environment
5. ________________ energy-efficient lightbulbs that are better for the environment
6. ________________ logging by certifying forests
7. ________________ the number of jobs in development and production of renewables
8. ________________ carbon emissions

B Read the descriptions below and scan the passage to find the relevant sections. Then give an example for each description.

UNDERSTANDING PROBLEMS AND SOLUTIONS

1. how sustainable communities help the environment

   ____

2. how livestock production facilities harm the environment

   ____

3. the type of activity that a socially responsible company might engage in

   ____

4. one problem logging causes

   ____

5. an industry that provides green employment

   ____

6. a country that is trying to cut down on CO_2 emissions

   ____

INTERPRETING VISUAL INFORMATION

C Answer these questions about the infographic in the reading passage.

1. What does the infographic show?
   a. the world leaders in renewable energy around the world
   b. the amount of money spent on renewable energy
   c. the best places in the world to invest in renewable energy
2. Which of the eight steps in the reading does the infographic relate to? ____________
3. Which two countries are world leaders in more than one energy type?

   ____
4. Which country is in the top five for all the energy types?

   ____
5. Overall, which country has the highest capacity for renewable power?

   ____

INFERRING MEANING

D Find and underline the following words and phrases in **bold** in the reading passage. Use context to identify their meanings. Write your own definitions and share them with a partner.

1. **tax break** (paragraph E):

   ____
2. **harvesting** (paragraph F):

   ____
3. **market share** (paragraph H):

   ____
4. **jointly** (paragraph J):

   ____

UNDERSTANDING APPOSITIVES

E Scan paragraphs F and I for examples of appositives. Underline the appositive and circle the noun or noun phrase that it refers to.

CRITICAL THINKING: EVALUATING

F Work in groups. In your opinion, which three steps in the passage are the most important? List them and share your reasons with your group.

1. ____________ 2. ____________ 3. ____________

I think ... is the most important step as ...

That's true, but I think ... will have a greater impact because ...

Writing

EXPLORING WRITTEN ENGLISH

A Read the sentences below. In which sentence does the underlined part just give extra information—information that is not essential for the sentence? Discuss your answer with a partner. NOTICING

1. We need to vote for leaders <u>who understand the serious issues impacting our climate</u>.
2. Together, these factors contribute to rising sea levels, <u>which could rise by three feet by 2100</u>.
3. Animals and plants are already vanishing from parts of their range <u>that are now too hot</u>.

LANGUAGE FOR WRITING Using Adjective Clauses

Adjective clauses give additional information about nouns in sentences. They can be either restrictive or nonrestrictive.

Restrictive adjective clauses give essential information about a noun. If you delete the adjective clause, you don't know which specific person or thing the sentence is about. These adjective clauses can begin with the relative pronouns *who* (for people) and *that* (for things and people). Do not use commas with restrictive clauses.

*The man <u>**who** wrote the article</u> is an environmentalist.* (The restrictive clause tells us which man.)

*One source of energy <u>**that** China uses</u> is wind power.* (The restrictive clause gives essential information.)

Nonrestrictive adjective clauses give extra information about a noun—information that isn't necessary or essential to identify the noun. Using nonrestrictive adjective clauses is a good way to add details to your sentences and make your writing more interesting. These adjective clauses can begin with the relative pronouns *who* (for people) and *which* (for things). Use commas with nonrestrictive adjective clauses.

*Metal ores, <u>**which** we use to manufacture goods</u>, are nonrenewable resources.* (The nonrestrictive clause gives more details about metal ores.)

*It's time for investors, <u>**who** do not always consider the effects of their investments</u>, to become more environmentally conscious.* (The nonrestrictive clause gives more details about the investors.)

USING RESTRICTIVE ADJECTIVE CLAUSES

B **Combine the sentences using restrictive adjective clauses.**

Example: Companies had to pay a fine. The companies dumped waste into a nearby lake.

Companies that dumped waste into a nearby lake had to pay a fine.

1. Farms can increase the risk of dangerous diseases—such as avian flu—spreading. The farms are close to city centers.

2. The Thai government placed a high tax on poultry farms. The poultry farms were within 100 kilometers of Bangkok.

3. Sun and wind power are two energy sources. Sun and wind power are renewable.

USING NONRESTRICTIVE ADJECTIVE CLAUSES

C **Use nonrestrictive adjective clauses to add extra information to the sentences.**

1. Beef production contributes to climate change. It requires a lot of water.

2. The city of Curitiba has very little traffic congestion. Curitiba has an efficient bus system.

3. Leonardo DiCaprio has produced a documentary on climate change. He is a UN Messenger of Peace.

WRITING SKILL Writing an Opinion Essay

When you write an opinion essay, you express your feelings about an issue and give reasons to explain your opinion.

The thesis statement states your opinion and your reasons. You can include an opinion expression in your thesis statement, such as *In my opinion, I think, I believe, From my point of view,* and *From my perspective.*

In my opinion, two effective ways to minimize the effects of climate change are to reduce carbon emissions from factories and to make people aware of the problem.

Each body paragraph includes a topic sentence that gives a reason. It also includes details, examples, and facts that explain the reason.

D Look at the outline for an opinion essay. Note answers to the questions below and discuss with a partner.

ANALYZING

1. What issue is the writer expressing an opinion about?

   ____

2. What is the writer's opinion?

   ____

3. What are the two main reasons the writer gives for their opinion?

   ____

4. What are some ways the writer will explain the first reason? The second reason?

   ____

   ____

Introductory Paragraph	
Hook / Background Information	overconsumption of resources; need to change habits
Thesis Statement	In my opinion, becoming a vegetarian is the best way to preserve our resources and slow down global warming because it saves water and cuts down on carbon emissions.
Body Paragraphs	
Topic Sentence 1	One reason that vegetarianism is a good way to reduce our use of resources is that it saves large amounts of water.
Details	• meat production uses a lot of water; e.g., beef production: 1 kg of beef = 16,000L • plant production uses much less; e.g., 1 kg of rice = 3,400L; 1 kg of corn = 833L
Topic Sentence 2	Another reason that becoming a vegetarian is good for the planet is that it helps to slow down global warming.
Details	• meat production ⟶ greenhouse gases ⟶ more than cars • meat production uses a lot of fossil fuels (to run production facilities; to transport, process, and refrigerate meat)
Concluding Paragraph	
Summary Statement	Not eating meat is a good way to ensure a sustainable future because it uses less water and it doesn't contribute as much to greenhouse gases.
Final Thought	veg diet ⟶ healthy planet, healthy people

REVISING PRACTICE

The draft below is an opinion essay about vegetarianism. Follow the steps to create a better second draft.

1. Add these sentences (a–c) in paragraphs **B–D** to provide extra information.
   a. One reason that vegetarianism is a good way to reduce our use of resources is that it saves large amounts of water.
   b. Besides being good for the planet, vegetarianism has some additional benefits.
   c. In fact, according to a United Nations report, raising animals for food produces more greenhouse gases than cars.
2. Now fix the following problems (d–f) in the essay.
   d. Add this restrictive clause to paragraph A: *that heat up the planet*
   e. Add this nonrestrictive clause to paragraph A: *, which all living things need to survive,*
   f. Cross out a sentence that doesn't belong in paragraph B.

A

It's a fact that we're using more of Earth's resources than nature can replenish. For example, fresh water _____ is becoming scarce. In addition, lifestyle habits _____ are causing climate change. What's the answer? In my opinion, becoming a vegetarian is the best way to preserve our resources and slow down global warming because it saves water and cuts down on carbon emissions.

B

_____ Meat production, which involves raising animals and processing them to turn them into edible products, is very water intensive. For example, it takes 16,000 liters of water to produce just one kilogram of beef. By comparison, it takes only 3,400 liters of water to produce a kilogram of rice, and a mere 833 liters to produce the same amount of corn. Producing biofuels from corn and other plants also uses large amounts of water.

C

Another reason that becoming a vegetarian is good for the planet is that it helps to slow down global warming. Meat production emits greenhouse gases such as CO_2. Trees, which absorb CO_2, are often cut down to make room for grazing animals. In addition, meat production uses a lot of fossil fuels to run production facilities and to transport meat products. These fossil fuels contribute to greenhouse gases. _____ By not eating meat, we might be able to slow down climate change.

D

Not eating meat is a good way to ensure a sustainable future because it uses less water, and it also reduces greenhouse gas emissions. _____ Studies show that a vegetarian diet, which tends to be low in fat, leads to a lower risk of heart disease. It also reduces the risk of other serious diseases such as cancer. By becoming vegetarians, we will ensure the health of the planet and our own health at the same time.

EDITING PRACTICE

Read the information below.

In sentences with adjective clauses, remember to:

- use commas before and after a nonrestrictive adjective clause if it is in the middle of the sentence.
- use *who* for people and *which* for things in nonrestrictive adjective clauses.
- use *who* for people and *that* for people or things in restrictive clauses.

Correct one mistake with adjective clauses in each of the sentences (1–6).

1. Vegetarianism which means not eating meat, is one way to reduce greenhouse gas emissions.
2. CFLs, that are popular in countries like Japan, use 75 percent less energy than traditional lightbulbs.
3. Logging which is done without regulation causes many types of environmental harm.
4. Costa Rica, which already generates 80 percent of its energy through renewable sources has promised to have zero net carbon emissions by 2030.
5. DiCaprio, which is the founder of the Leonardo DiCaprio Foundation, is working to make people aware of the effects of climate change.
6. DiCaprio made a film, that gave people a sense of urgency.

UNIT REVIEW

Answer the following questions.

1. Which of the ideas in the unit do you think is the best approach for achieving a sustainable future? Why?

____

____

____

2. What is the difference between restrictive and nonrestrictive adjective clauses?

____

____

____

3. Do you remember the meanings of these words? Check (✓) the ones you know. Look back at the unit and review the ones you don't know.

Reading 1:

☐ crucial AWL ☐ currently ☐ exceptional
☐ focus on AWL ☐ generate AWL ☐ practical
☐ related to ☐ shrink ☐ vanish
☐ worldwide

Reading 2:

☐ consume AWL ☐ convert AWL ☐ cut down on
☐ emit ☐ exhaust ☐ invest AWL
☐ limited ☐ major AWL ☐ reduction
☐ regulate AWL

Unit
2 Argument Essays

A winding highway in New Taipei City on the island of Taiwan

OBJECTIVES To learn how to write an argument essay
To use effective transitions and connectors in argument writing
To understand the important role of modals in argument essays
To learn how to use *-ly* adverbs of degree in advanced writing

Should a driver's license ever be taken away due to age?

What Is an Argument Essay?

We frequently attempt to persuade others to agree with our viewpoints, such as which movie to watch or where to go on vacation. In writing an **argument essay**, we use written words to achieve a similar goal. In argument essays, sometimes referred to as persuasive essays, writers attempt to convince their readers to agree with them on a particular issue. By explaining their reasons for holding a particular belief, writers hope to sway others to share their point of view or to take a particular action. For example, in an argument essay about why people should recycle, you might explain two or three reasons that recycling is good for the environment. After giving these reasons for recycling, you should present an opinion that people who do not recycle might say, such as "One person cannot make a difference." Your response to that opposing opinion could then include data showing how much garbage one person produces per year and how much of that could be recycled.

One type of argument essay is a newspaper or magazine editorial where writers choose an issue and explain its relevance to their readers to create a community of like-minded thinkers. For example, an editorial writer might endorse a particular candidate in an election, with the hope of persuading readers to vote for the candidate the writer thinks will do the best job. We strongly recommend reading an editorial in a newspaper of your choice to help you understand what argument writing is. In fact, you should read editorials in a few different newspapers or similar sources to become familiar with the writing style and organization of good argument writing.

Another type of argument essay writing appears in blogs as the blog writer explains his or her reasons for supporting or disagreeing with a certain issue. Of course not all blog entries are persuasive writing, but many are in fact very good examples with well-supported opinions.

Well-written and organized argument essays clearly and logically explain a writer's reasons behind a given viewpoint. However, writers should not exaggerate their claims. It is better to be candid about the limitations of their viewpoint than to overstate the case. If their arguments seem exaggerated or untrue, readers will distrust the writers and not accept their ideas.

How Is an Argument Essay Organized?

Your goal in an argument essay is to convince your readers that your opinion about an issue (your thesis statement) is valid and important. To accomplish this goal, your essay must state your opinion about the issue clearly. However, your essay also needs to be balanced to show that you understand the issue completely. One way to do this is to include an opposing viewpoint, or **counterargument**. Even though you are arguing one side of an issue (either *for* or *against*), you must think about what someone on the other side of the issue would argue. After giving your opponent's point of view, you offer a **refutation**. This means that you refute the other point of view, or show how it is wrong. Discussing only your opinion makes your essay sound biased, and your readers may not be convinced of your viewpoint.

An argument essay is organized in the same general manner as the other essays in this book.

- It begins with an **introductory paragraph** that introduces the topic and thesis of the essay.
- The **body paragraphs** discuss the pros and cons of the thesis statement. As with all types of essays, the body paragraphs have supporting information.
- An argument essay often contains a **counterargument**, which is an opposing opinion, in the body of the essay. This counterargument is presented, explained, and then suggested to be untrue or less important in the **refutation**.
- The **conclusion** summarizes the main points of the argument and restates the writer's thesis.

In a five-paragraph essay, one way to organize the body paragraphs is for paragraphs two and three to provide support for your thesis, and then for paragraph four to introduce and refute a counterargument. However, the number of body paragraphs can be as few as two or as many as necessary to explain your position. For example, if you are writing a five-paragraph essay in which you argue that people should recycle as much as they can, paragraphs two and three could give reasons to support your thesis. Then paragraph four could present the opposing idea that recycling is ineffective, along with a refutation of that opposing idea. Such an essay might look like this

<table>
<tr><td>INTRODUCTION</td><td>Paragraph 1</td><td>Hook
Connecting information
Thesis</td></tr>
<tr><td rowspan="3">BODY</td><td>Paragraph 2</td><td>Support 1: Recycling saves energy.
• Creating glass from recycled glass uses 50 percent less energy than making new glass.
• Recycling one can of soda saves enough energy to run a TV for three hours.</td></tr>
<tr><td>Paragraph 3</td><td>Support 2: Recycling reduces air pollution.
• Using recycled products helps reduce the amount of pollution in our air.</td></tr>
<tr><td>Paragraph 4</td><td>Opposing viewpoint(s)
• Counterargument: One person cannot make a difference.
• Refutation: Each person produces 1,600 pounds of waste each year, but as much as 1,100 pounds of that total could be recycled.</td></tr>
<tr><td>CONCLUSION</td><td>Paragraph 5</td><td>Restated thesis
Suggestion/opinion/prediction</td></tr>
</table>

Writer's Note

Many Essays Are Argument Writing

Other essay types—process, comparison, and cause-effect—can also be seen as argument essays. A process essay could attempt to persuade the reader that the process being described is the most appropriate means of achieving a desired result. A comparison essay might recommend one choice above another, and use the comparison points as arguments. A cause-effect essay could argue that a certain event or course of action is harmful because of its effects. When you write in any rhetorical mode, persuasion can still be one of your goals. You want your reader to share your view of the world around you.

Great Topics for Argument Essays

What is a great topic for an argument essay? Obviously, it should be an issue that you feel strongly about, know something about, and would like to share your opinions on. What is your opinion on the issue? Why do you feel this way? Can you think of some reasons why people might think differently than you do?

When selecting topics for this type of essay, consider relevant questions such as:

- Does the topic have two (or more) viewpoints? A topic without at least two viewpoints is not suitable.
- How much do you know about this topic? You should choose a topic that you know about and feel passionately about.

As you read this list of general topics that lend themselves well to an argument essay, ask yourself what your opinion is about the topic. Can you also think of at least one opposing viewpoint for each topic?

General Topics for Argument	
limiting oil exploration in environmentally sensitive areas	requiring a test for people who want to have children
legalizing capital punishment	raising the driving age
mandating military service	using animals for medical research
requiring school uniforms	getting rid of zoos
banning cigarettes	rating or restricting video games

ACTIVITY 1 Identifying Topics for Argument Essays

Read these eight topics. Put a check mark (✓) next to the four that could be good topics for argument essays.

_______ **1.** The first time I flew in a plane

_______ **2.** The choice of a specific candidate to vote for in an election

_______ **3.** How and why birds migrate south for the winter

_______ **4.** Steps in negotiating an international contract

_______ **5.** The necessity of higher taxes on gasoline

________ **6.** Why schools should offer after-school programs for at-risk students

________ **7.** Reasons that you deserve a raise at your job

________ **8.** How to play chess well

Can you think of two additional topics that would be excellent for an argument essay?

9. ____________________

10. ____________________

Supporting Details

After you have selected a topic, think about what you already know about the issue and what you need to find out. Asking yourself questions about both sides of the issue is a good way to generate details to include in your essay.

When you brainstorm your plan for an argument essay, a useful technique is to fill in a pro-con chart with the pro points in favor of the thesis statement and the con points against the thesis statement. If you cannot generate many ideas for one or both sides, you need to do more research on the issue or choose a different issue.

Here is a pro-con chart for an essay arguing that people over age eighteen should (or should not) be required to vote:

Thesis Statement: Voting should be required by all citizens over eighteen.

Pro	Con
1. In a democracy, everyone should participate.	1. In a democracy, people should have the right to vote as well as not to vote.
2. In our history, many people have died in wars so that we can vote.	2. Some people do not know the candidates and do not want to make a decision.
3. If everyone votes, then the chosen candidate will represent the whole country.	3. Some people know the candidates and do not want to have to vote for any of them.

ACTIVITY 2 Brainstorming Supporting Ideas

Read the thesis statements and complete the pro-con charts. Write three ideas to support each statement. Then write three ideas against each statement. Finally, choose another topic and write a thesis statement and pro-con supports for your new topic.

1. *Thesis statement*: Adults should be required to pass a test before they can become parents.

Pro	Con
1.	1.
2.	2.
3.	3.

2. *Thesis statement*: The death penalty helps society to protect innocent people.

Pro	Con
1.	1.
2.	2.
3.	3.

3. *Your thesis statement*: ____________________

Pro	Con
1.	1.
2.	2.
3.	3.

ACTIVITY 3 Studying an Example Argument Essay

This essay suggests that studying abroad is a valuable experience for university students. Discuss the Preview Questions with a partner. Then read the essay and answer the questions that follow.

Preview Questions

1. If you were going to complete a semester abroad, where would you want to go? Explain your answer.
2. Can you think of three reasons that a student should study abroad? Can you think of three reasons that students should not study abroad? Complete the pro-con chart.

Thesis statement: All students should complete at least one semester abroad.

Pro	Con
1.	1.
2.	2.
3.	3.

3. Do you think colleges and universities should modify their graduation requirements to include the mandatory completion of at least one semester in a study-abroad program? Why or why not?

Essay 1

The Best Classroom

1 Because of such factors as the rise of the Internet, the ease of global travel, and a dramatic increase in international trade, the world is more interconnected than ever before. In the past, people could enjoy a successful career without ever moving from their home region, but now many people have jobs that involve some international interactions. **Given** these new conditions, it is essential that all college and university students experience new cultures as part of their education. To achieve this objective and to emphasize the importance of intercultural studies, colleges and universities should require students to study abroad for at least one semester of their undergraduate education.

2 One of the primary reasons that studying abroad contributes so effectively to students' education is that it requires them to live and learn in a new culture that is different from their **upbringing**. In their analysis of the educational benefits of study-abroad programs, Brewer and Cunningham (2009) conclude that real learning is often **triggered** by a serious **dilemma** that causes the individuals involved to question

given: because of; due to

upbringing: the way or manner in which a child is raised by parents or caregivers

to trigger: to cause to happen

a dilemma: a choice between two things that are equally good or bad

assumptions they may have held for their entire lives (p. 9). As Brewer and Cunningham demonstrate, students' daily assumptions are challenged by the experience of living abroad, from simple concerns, such as appropriate breakfast foods, to more complex matters, such as how societies should be organized and other cultural conventions. By experiencing a new culture firsthand, students will better appreciate the unique features of both their host and their home countries, as well as better understand the **repercussions** of these cultural differences.

3 Studying abroad also greatly **facilitates** learning a new language. While students should prepare to study abroad by learning this language in the classroom, thereby establishing a **framework** for future success, few experiences **enhance** language learning more than living in a country where it is used. As Kauffmann, Martin, and Weaver (1992) state, "Foreign settings offer many new resources for instruction, practice, and evaluation. Teaching methods that take advantage of the local environments can certainly be expected to improve on classroom methods" (p. 36). For example, when learning a new language in a classroom, students might practice ordering food at a restaurant or asking directions to a museum; when studying abroad, however, they will have to put these skills to the test in real-world situations.

4 Additionally, students benefit from studying their academic **discipline** from a new perspective. At first, this argument may appear illogical: math is math, whether in Peru or Poland, and the **fundamental** principles of chemistry do not change from Ghana to Germany. Still, the ways in which disciplines are organized and taught may vary **considerably** from one region to another, and so students will see their discipline **in a new light** if it is taught in even a slightly different method or order. Learning to see the ways in which knowledge itself is organized can be one of the greatest benefits of studying abroad.

5 Though studying abroad offers many advantages, some may argue that a semester or a year abroad is nothing but a vacation. Yes, it is true that some students choose to treat studying abroad as a vacation rather than the rich academic experience that it can be. The bad actions of a few students should not **invalidate** study abroad programs as a whole or cause colleges to abandon their efforts in this regard. In fact, in a long-term study of 3,400 students, Dwyer and Peters (2004) found that a large number said studying abroad had an impact on their world view (96 percent), increased their self-confidence (96 percent), and gave them the skill sets they needed for the career they chose (76 percent). Clearly, studying abroad is not just a party. Students' home institutions should offer preparatory workshops and orientation seminars so that students will be ready for the requirements of the program and will better understand how it connects with their current academic work. Studying abroad unites academic demands with the **thrill** of discovering a new culture, and students will gain immeasurably more from the experience if they are prepared prior to departure for what they will discover there.

an assumption: a belief or an opinion

a repercussion: a negative result that was not expected

to facilitate: to help; to make easier

a framework: a basic structure

to enhance: to make something better, easier, or more effective

a discipline: field of study; subject area

fundamental: basic; most important

considerably: a great amount; to a significant degree

in a new light: in a new way

to invalidate: to prove that something is not true

the thrill: the excitement

6 Given the numerous benefits of studying abroad, colleges and universities should require that their students take advantage of this opportunity, while also doing everything possible to keep these experiences affordable through reduced tuition and **subsidized** fees. It is essential that students learn to negotiate our increasingly interconnected world by exploring new cultures as part of their education. In a world made smaller by technological advances, students who graduate with the experience of living in a foreign culture will also be better prepared to succeed in their careers.

to subsidize: to help pay for the cost of something

References

Brewer, E., & Cunningham, K. (2009). Capturing study abroad's transformative potential. In E. Brewer & K. Cunningham (Eds.), *Integrating study abroad into the curriculum: Theory and practice across the disciplines* (pp. 1–29). Sterling, VA: Stylus.

Dwyer, M., & Peters, C. (2004). The benefits of study abroad. *Transitions Abroad, 27* (5), 56–57.

Kauffmann, N., Martin, J., & Weaver, H., with J. Weaver. (1992). *Students abroad, strangers at home: Education for a global society*. Yarmouth, ME: Intercultural Press.

Post-Reading Questions

1. How many paragraphs does this essay have? ______________________

2. What is the topic of the essay? ______________________

3. What is the writer's thesis? ______________________

____

4. What reasons does the writer give for her viewpoint?

____

____

____

5. After reading this student's essay, do you agree with the thesis? Why or why not?

____

____

____

6. If you answered *no* to the previous question, answer a. If you answered *yes*, answer b.

a. If you disagree with the thesis, what could the writer have done to make her point more convincing?

____

____

____

b. If you agree with the thesis, what are some ways in which the writer could have been even more convincing?

____

____

____

7. Does the last sentence in the conclusion offer a suggestion, an opinion, or a prediction?

____

Building Better Vocabulary

ACTIVITY 4 Practicing Three Kinds of Vocabulary from Context

Read each important vocabulary word or phrase. Locate it in the essay if you need help remembering the word or phrase. Then circle the best synonym, antonym, or collocation from column A, B, or C.

Type of Vocabulary	Important Vocabulary	A	B	C
Synonyms	**1.** trigger	arrange	cause	enter
	2. assess	leave	persuade	test
	3. dilemma	liquid	necessity	problem
	4. impact	effect	knowledge	view
Antonyms	**5.** abroad	distant	local	weak
	6. repercussion	cause	individual	mastery
	7. complex	frequent	necessary	simple
	8. affordable	believable	expensive	honest
Collocations	**9.** ___ abroad	hear	mention	study
	10. my current ___	quickness	situation	upbringing
	11. ___ for granted	look	make	take
	12. vary ___	calmly	considerably	well

ACTIVITY 5 Analyzing the Organization

Use the words from the box to complete the outline of "The Best Classroom." Reread the essay on pages 31–33 if you need help.

- To achieve this objective, colleges and universities should require students to study abroad for at least one semester of their undergraduate education.
- Consider the real-world language situations in which students have to operate every day.
- Demonstrate that study abroad improves students' lives.
- Suggest that seeing new ways to organize knowledge is a major outcome of studying abroad.
- Offer a prediction
- Show how studying abroad teaches students about not only the foreign culture but also their own culture.

Title: The Best Classroom

I. Introduction

A. The world is a smaller place.

B. People's jobs now depend on international connections.

C. Thesis statement: ______________________________.

II. Body Paragraph 1

A. Show how studying abroad makes students experience a foreign culture.

B. ______________________________.

III. Body Paragraph 2

A. Discuss how studying abroad contributes to learning a foreign language.

B. ______________________________.

IV. Body Paragraph 3

A. Explain how studying abroad allows students to see their academic discipline from a new perspective.

B. ______________________________.

V. Body Paragraph 4

A. Address a common opposing idea that studying abroad is just a vacation.

B. Prove that A is not accurate here: ______________________________.

C. Argue that schools need to prepare their students for study abroad so they know the requirements and goals.

VI. Conclusion

A. Suggest that studying abroad should be required.

B. ______________________ about the future lives of students who graduate from a college or university that has a required study abroad component.

Strong Thesis Statements for Argument Essays

A strong thesis statement for an argument essay states a clear position on the issue. The thesis often includes a word or phrase that signals an opinion, such as **should**, **ought to**, **need to**, **have an obligation to**, or even **must** or **had better**.

In addition, a thesis statement sometimes uses general phrases such as **for a number of reasons**, **for a number of important reasons**, or **in many ways**. Sometimes a thesis statement may list the actual reasons for supporting or opposing an idea or say how many reasons will be discussed in the paper.

Finally, a thesis statement can use hedging words such as **some** or **some people** as well as **may**, **might**, **can**, **seem**, or **appear** with the verb to limit or qualify an unsupported statement. These thesis statements often use a contrasting connector such as **although**, **while**, or **despite**.

Type of thesis	Example thesis statement
simple thesis	It is easy to demonstrate that pets help humans **in many ways**. School uniforms **should** be required **for three reasons**.
stronger thesis, listing reasons	College students **should** be encouraged to pursue a career in science because of **the large number of job options** and **the higher salaries**. Taxes are a necessary part of our society; without them, we could not pay for **our roads and bridges** or **our schools**.
stronger thesis including possible counterargument	**Although some** may object to the death penalty, this punishment is a necessity to **control public order** and **ensure people's safety**. **While some people** think paying taxes is unfair, all of us **should** pay taxes because we all benefit from **what they provide in our daily lives**.

- The thesis statement for an argument essay cannot be a fact. A fact is not a good topic for this kind of essay because a fact cannot be argued. For example, "the number of people in the United States" is not controversial. "The population of the United States is increasing every year" is not a good thesis statement because it is a fact, and there is no way to argue this point.
- A thesis statement should not be a personal opinion that cannot be proved. For example, "Popcorn is more delicious than peanuts" cannot be proved because this is based on one person's opinion.
- The thesis statement must state or imply a position on the issue, and the position should be very clear. For the topic of "cigarette smoking," a possible thesis statement is "The manufacture of cigarettes should be stopped." In contrast, the statement "Cigarette smoking isn't a very good idea" is too vague and general to be a thesis.

ACTIVITY 6 Writing Strong Thesis Statements for Argument Essays

Write a pro thesis statement and a con thesis statement for each topic. When you finish, compare your answers with a partner's.

1. Topic: University education for everyone

Pro thesis statement: ______________________________

____

Con thesis statement: ______________________________

____

2. Topic: Paying professional athletes extremely high salaries

Pro thesis statement: ____

____

Con thesis statement: ____

____

3. Topic: Using alternative energy sources

Pro thesis statement: ____

____

Con thesis statement: ____

____

Strong Counterargument and Refutation Statements for Argument Essays

The most important technique in persuading readers that your viewpoint is valid is to support it in every paragraph, but another strong technique is to write a good **counterargument** that goes against your thesis statement. Introducing this counterargument adds credibility to your essay. It shows that you understand more than one point of view about your topic.

After you provide a counterargument, you must give a **refutation**, or a response to the counterargument, that either disproves it or shows it to be weaker or less important than your point.

In simple terms, imagine that you are having an argument with a friend about your topic. She disagrees with your opinion. What do you think will be her strongest argument against your point of view? That is your counterargument. How will you respond to her counterargument? Your answer is your refutation.

Look at the following excerpt from "The Best Classroom" on pages 31–33. The counterargument is in italics and the refutation is underlined.

> Though studying abroad offers many advantages, *some may argue that a semester or a year abroad is nothing but a vacation.* Yes, it is true that some students choose to treat studying abroad as a vacation rather than the rich academic experience that it can be. The bad actions of a few students should not invalidate study-abroad programs as a whole. In fact, <u>in a long-term study of 3,400 students,</u> Dwyer and Peters (2004) found <u>that a large number said studying abroad had an impact on their world view (96 percent), increased their self-confidence (96 percent), and gave them the skill sets they needed for the career they chose (76 percent). Clearly, studying abroad is not just a party</u>.

As you can see, what begins as a counterargument ends up as another reason in support of the writer's opinion.

ACTIVITY 7 Writing Refutations for Counterarguments

For each counterargument, write a one-sentence refutation. Remember to use a contrasting connection word (*although, while, despite*) to begin your refutation.

1. Topic: Mandatory retirement for pilots

   Thesis statement: Pilots should be required to retire at age 60 to ensure the safety of passengers.

   Counterargument: Some people may believe that older pilots' experience can contribute to flight safety.

   Refutation: While this may be true for a handful of pilots, the vast majority of people report weaker eyesight, hearing, and motor skills as they age.

2. Topic: National identity cards

   Thesis statement: A national identity card would make life better for everyone, especially when voting, applying for a job, or paying taxes.

   Counterargument: Some people might oppose national identity cards because they are afraid of the government having too much control in their daily lives.

   Refutation: ______________________________

3. Topic: Teachers' salaries

   Thesis statement: Teachers' salaries should be tied to their students' test scores.

   Counterargument: Some people may believe that a teacher's role in a student's test score is not that important.

   Refutation: ______________________________

Transitions and Connectors in Argument Essays

Transitional phrases and connectors in argument essays help the reader to follow the logical development of the argument. These transitions can be used to connect sentences, ideas, and paragraphs. Here are some common transitions and connectors for developing support in your argument and for addressing a counterargument.

Transitions and Connectors That Develop a Point Further			
additionally	correspondingly	furthermore	moreover
also	for example	in a similar manner	similarly
besides	for instance	likewise	what is more

Transitions and Connectors That Address a Counterargument			
although	even though	nevertheless	still
but	however	nonetheless	though
conversely	in contrast	on the other hand	while
despite	in spite of	some people might say	yet

ACTIVITY 8 Identifying Transitions and Connectors in an Argument Essay

Reread "The Best Classroom" on pages 31–33. Find seven transitions or connectors. Copy the sentences here, underline the transition or connector, and write the paragraph number in the parentheses.

Transitions/Connectors That Develop a Point Further

1. ____

____ ( )

2. ____

____ ( )

3. ____

____ ( )

Transitions/Connectors That Address a Counterargument

1. ____

____ ( )

2. ____

____ ( )

3. ____

____ ( )

4. ____

____ ( )

Studying Transitions and Connectors in an Example Argument Essay

ACTIVITY 9 Warming Up to the Topic

Answer the questions on your own. Then discuss them with a partner or in a small group.

1. What does the term *overfishing* mean? ____

____

2. Do a quick Internet search for the term *overfishing*. Write three facts that you learn.

____

____

____

3. What are some possible solutions to the problem of overfishing?

____

____

____

4. What is a fish farm? Are there any fish farms located near where you live?

____

____

____

ACTIVITY 10 Using Transitions and Connectors in an Essay

Read "Empty Oceans" and circle the correct transition words or phrases.

Essay 2

Empty Oceans

1 Imagine going to a sushi restaurant that could no longer serve fish. Such a scenario may seem very difficult to believe, but the fish populations of the earth's oceans face severe threats. Like land animals that have been hunted to near extinction, such as buffalo, elephants, and tigers, marine

animals also need to be protected if they are to survive into future generations. Governments **1** (encourage / must encourage) **sustainable** fishing practices and other regulatory guidelines to ensure that the oceans preserve their variety of animal and plant life as well as sufficient fish populations.

sustainable: able to continue to use longer; continuing for future generations

2 The oceans are being **depleted** primarily due to consumer demand for seafood, which creates a financial **incentive** for marine businesses to overfish. As National Geographic documents, "Demand for seafood and advances in technology have led to fishing practices that are depleting fish and shellfish populations around the world. Fishers remove more than 77 billion kilograms (170 billion pounds) of wildlife from the sea each year." Similarly, Pichegru and her colleagues (2012) researched the challenges facing fish populations due to industrial fishing, concluding that "the development of industrial fishing in the twentieth century has reduced the total number of predatory fish globally to less than ten-percent of pre-industrial levels . . . and profoundly altered marine environments" (p. 117). Because of this enormous reduction, many species of fish and shellfish cannot reproduce quickly enough to **compensate for** the numbers that have been removed, which further **compounds** the problem.

to deplete: to use up; to finish all of something

an incentive: a reason or motivation to do something

to compensate for: to make up for; to substitute for

to compound: to make something worse

3 **2** (Despite / What is more), shifting ocean environments have made it very difficult for many fish to find enough prey to feed upon, and without a sufficient food supply, their population growth can be severely limited. Overfishing causes many other problems in the oceans. Changing the oceanic environment drastically multiplies the challenges that sea creatures face, as evidenced by such factors as the **collapse** of coral reefs in oceans throughout the world and other such worrisome trends.

collapse: destruction; breakdown

4 **3** (As a result / While) some people may **downplay** the problem of overfishing of our oceans, the statistics confirm its **gravity**. The number of fish is decreasing, and fishermen have to go farther and farther to find fish to catch. Stronger government controls of the fishing industry would help limit overfishing. **4** (Additionally / On one hand), tax breaks could be given to companies that operate fish

to downplay: to minimize the importance of something

gravity: a very serious quality or condition

farms, which are perhaps one of the simplest solutions to this problem. Rather than taking fish and shellfish from the ocean, fish farmers build unique facilities, such as tanks, aquariums, and other **marine enclosures**, to raise these animals. 5 (Before / While) fish farming may be unfamiliar to many people, the practice dates back to 2000 B.C.E. in China, and its training manuals include a 475 B.C.E. essay on raising carp by Fan Lai (Shepherd and Bromage, 1992, p. 2). With modern advancements in technology, fish farming promises to **revolutionize** how humans fish.

marine: having to do with the ocean

an enclosure: an area or container for keeping animals

to revolutionize: to change in a significant way

5 Because the oceans are huge, most people have not thought about oceans without fish. 6 (Because / Nevertheless), the fish in our oceans are in real trouble. In 1992, the United Nations Conference on Environment and Development defined the goal of sustainable development as meeting the "needs of the present without limiting the ability of future generations to meet their own needs" (Caulfield, 1997, p. 167). Without practical responses to the issue of sustainable fishing, including the necessity of **suspending** certain fishing practices and monitoring the health of the oceans, the planet risks losing many species of marine wildlife. By limiting fishing in the oceans and developing commercial fish farms, we can succeed in both raising fish for human consumption and preserving fish for the future.

to suspend: to stop something, usually for a short time

References

Caulfield, R. (1997). *Greenlanders, whales, and whaling: Sustainability and self-determination in the Arctic*. Hanover, NH: University Press of New England.

Pichegru, L., Ryan, P., van Eeden, R., Reid, T., Grémillet, D., & Wanless, R. (2012). Industrial fishing, no-take zones and endangered penguins. *Biological Conservation, 156*, 117–125.

Shepherd, J., & Bromage, N. (1992). *Intensive fish farming*. Oxford: Blackwell Science.

Sustainable fishing. National Geographic Education, (n.d.) Retrieved from http://education.nationalgeographic.com/education/encyclopedia/sustainable-fishing/?ar_a=1

Building Better Vocabulary

ACTIVITY 11 Practicing Three Kinds of Vocabulary from Context

Read each important vocabulary word or phrase. Locate it in the essay if you need help remembering the word or phrase. Then circle the best synonym, antonym, or collocation from column A, B, or C.

Type of Vocabulary	Important Vocabulary	A	B	C
Synonyms	**1.** a colleague	a co-worker	a friend	an incident
	2. enormous	fancy	gloomy	huge
	3. alter	change	imagine	vanish
	4. preserve	join	protect	serve
Antonyms	**5.** a solution	an answer	an opinion	a problem
	6. unique	common	purchase	respond
	7. deplete	need	increase	omit
	8. downplay	emphasize	revolutionize	suggest
Collocations	**9.** ___ limited	happily	next	severely
	10. a vast ___	entry	family	number
	11. ___ than	essential	given	rather
	12. a ___ incentive	financial	kind	population

Grammar for Writing

Modals

Modals are words that are used together with verbs. Modals express ability, possibility, or obligation, and are very important in writing because they change the tone of a sentence. For example, modals such as **must** and **had better** make a verb sound stronger, while modals such as **may**, **might**, **should**, **can**, and **could** make a verb softer, weaker, or less certain.

Modals play a special role in argument essays because writers need to state a clear opinion about the topic. In this case, strong modals such as *must* and *had better* help writers assert their main point and tell readers that something has to happen. Another very useful modal is *should*. Although *should* is not quite as strong as *must* or *had better*, it gives a clear recommendation or assertion and is therefore often used in argument essays:

Clear assertion: The sale of cigarettes **should** be banned immediately.

In addition, writers of argument essays need to acknowledge opposing opinions and then provide a refutation of that opinion. Modals such as *may, might, could,* and *can* help writers make an opposing opinion sound weak. In particular, the use of *may* and *might* weakens the opposing viewpoint. The use of key modals is essential in constructing a well-written counterargument and refutation.

Clear opposing opinion: Although the new law banning smoking in restaurants **may** have been passed with good intentions, citizens **have to** realize that the government has overstepped its powers here.

Meaning	Examples
advisability	The sale of cigarettes **should** be banned immediately. Companies **ought to** supply health insurance to all employees. People **had better** realize that the plan to increase taxes will cause problems in their daily lives.
possibility	Students' test scores **may** increase if students spend at least thirty minutes per day writing. The effect of global warming **might** be reduced if pollution controls are passed. Doubling the price of fatty foods **could** reduce public consumption of these unhealthy foods.
certainty	Implementing the proposed changes in health care **will** result in a much healthier population.
necessity	For these reasons, the minimum age to obtain a driver's license **must** be raised immediately. Although the new law banning smoking in restaurants may have been passed with good intentions, citizens **have to** realize that the government has overstepped its powers here.

The verb after a modal is always in the base, or simple, form with no inflected ending (*-ing, -ed, -en, -s*). In addition, do not put the word *to* between the modal and the verb (unless *to* is part of the modal).

✗ The solution **might** lies in obtaining better raw materials.

✗ The solution **might** to lie in obtaining better raw materials.

✓ The solution **might lie** in obtaining better raw materials.

ACTIVITY 12 Working with Modals

Circle the six modals in this paragraph. Find the two errors and write the corrections above the errors.

Paragraph 1

A Trick for Remembering New Words

The task of learning and remembering new vocabulary words can be difficult. However, one technique that works very well for many students is the "key-word method." In this technique, learners must first to select a word in their native language that looks or sounds like the target English word. Then they should form a mental association or picture between the English word and the native-language word. For example, an English speaker learning the Malay word for door, *pintu*, might associating this target word with the English words *pin* and *into*. The learner would then visualize someone putting a "pin into a door" to open it. This could help the learner to remember *pintu* for door. Research on second-language learning shows that this technique consistently results in a very high level of learning.

Grammar for Writing

-ly Adverbs of Degree

One way to make your writing more precise, more formal, and more advanced is to use **adverbs of degree** before adjectives (and other adverbs). Some common examples include **very**, **really**, **so**, and **too**; however, ***-ly* adverbs of degree** are more common in writing. The form of these adverbs of degree is easy to learn: they end in *-ly*.

Adverbs of degree give information about the extent of something. They occur most often before adjectives, especially past participles used as adjectives. Instead of using common words *very* and *really* in your essays, make your writing more original and more advanced by using other adverbs of degree.

Common *-ly* Adverbs of Degree			
absolutely	especially	internationally	simply
adequately	extremely	partially	strongly
completely	fully	particularly	thoroughly
decidedly	greatly	perfectly	totally
deeply	hardly	practically	tremendously
enormously	highly	profoundly	utterly
entirely	immensely	scarcely	virtually

-ly Adverbs of Degree + _____	Examples
adverb of degree + adjective	Online courses are **immensely** popular.
adverb of degree + past participle as adjective	Tracy Jenks is an **internationally** recognized expert in antiterrorism.
adverb of degree + adverb of manner	Teachers today are under pressure to cover material in certain courses **extremely** quickly.

ACTIVITY 13 Working with *-ly* Adverbs of Degree

Unscramble the words and write each sentence correctly.

1. thoroughly / the speaker's remarks / was / by / the audience / disgusted

____

2. no longer / accurate / the medical tests / are / completely / used for heart disease

____

3. is that it is / about the weather / that we know / unpredictable / utterly / the sole fact

____

4. recognized as / was widely / the doctor / cancer research / an expert in

____

5. it was proven / dish was / although the / to be unhealthy / immensely popular,

____

6. to persuade / it can be / higher taxes / to vote for / difficult / citizens / extremely

____

ACTIVITY 14 Working with Adverbs

Circle the correct word in each set of parentheses.

Paragraph 2

Reporting Bad News

In a company, how should bad news be reported to employees? The 1 (bad / badly) news should be communicated up front in 2 (direct / directly) written messages. Even in an 3 (indirect / indirectly) written message, if you have done a 4 (convincing / convincingly) job of explaining the reasons, the bad news itself will 5 (natural / naturally) come as no surprise; the decision will appear 6 (logical / logically) and reasonable—indeed the only logical and 7 (reasonable / reasonably) decision that could have been made under the circumstances. Readers should not be 8 (tremendous / tremendously) shocked by any sudden news. To keep the reader's goodwill, state the bad news in 9 (positive / positively) or 10 (neutral / neutrally) language, stressing what you are able to do rather than what you are not able to do. In addition, put the bad news in the middle of a paragraph and include additional discussion of reasons in the same sentence or 11 (immediate / immediately) afterward. People may 12 (great / greatly) appreciate news that is delivered in this direct way, no matter how bad the news is.

ACTIVITY 15 Editing an Essay: Review of Grammar

Twelve of the sixteen words or phrases in parentheses contain an error involving one of the grammar topics featured in this unit. If the word or phrase is correct, write *C*. If it is incorrect, fill in the blank with a correction.

Essay 3

No More Spam

1 Spam, which Flynn and Kahn (2003) define as " 1 (unsolicited e-mail) ________________ that is neither wanted nor needed" (p. 179) by anyone, **threatens** the entire e-mail system. E-mail is a **vital** method of communication today, but the 2 (annoyingly mountain) ________________ of spam threatens to destroy this important **means** of modern communication. If e-mail is to continue to be useful, laws against

to threaten: to promise to harm somebody or something

vital: essential; very important

a means: a method; a way

spam (3) (may) ______________________ be strengthened and (4) (strictly **enforced**) ______________________ to avoid the **exploitation** of e-mail.

2 If the government does not act quickly to prevent the further increase of spam, the problem (5) (will certainly to get) ______________________ much worse. Computer programs allow spammers to send hundreds of millions of e-mails (6) (virtual **instantly**) ______________________. As more and more advertisers turn to spam to sell their products, the e-mail that people want to receive (7) (could to be) ______________________ greatly **outnumbered** by junk e-mail. Will people continue to use e-mail if (8) (they had to delete) ______________________ 100 pieces of spam for each personal e-mail they receive, and if the proportion of important e-mails becomes insignificant? It is estimated that "85 to 95 percent of all e-mail sent is spam," a problem that costs consumers and companies billions of dollars annually (Freeman, 2009, p. 120).

3 Although this problem with e-mail is **troubling** for private individuals, it is even worse for large businesses, which cannot ignore its harmful effects. Many spam e-mails contain computer viruses that

to enforce: to force someone to obey something

exploitation: the use of something unfairly for profit

instantly: immediately

to outnumber: to have a larger number than

troubling: worrying; disturbing

9 (can shut down) __________________ the entire network of a business. Companies rely on e-mail for their employees to communicate with one another. Spamming **corrupts** their internal communications, and can even cause equipment to **malfunction**, so that a company's employees are **10** (thus complete unable) __________________ to communicate effectively. Such a situation results in a loss of productivity for the company and sometimes requires the company to redesign its communication network. These computer problems raise the company's costs, **11** (which must) __________________ then be passed on to the consumer.

to corrupt: to cause to become bad or to not work

to malfunction: to not work properly

4 Despite these problems for individuals and businesses, some people **12** (should argue) __________________ that criminalizing spam limits spammers' right to free speech. However, how free is speech that **drowns out** other voices that people want to hear? Commercial speech that is designed to encourage people to spend money is **13** (legal differently) __________________ from people's right to voice their personal opinions. The right to free speech does not allow companies to flood computer inboxes with e-mail garbage. Yes, free speech is an **14** (essentially component) __________________ of the exchange of ideas necessary for any society and should not be restricted by unnecessary regulations. Unwanted e-mails, however, threaten to harm effective communication, not **nurture** it.

to drown out: to make it impossible to hear something

to nurture: to encourage to grow

5 Because of these important reasons, lawmakers **15** (may legislate) __________________ increased penalties or **levy** other types of fines or taxes against spam. Spammers **16** (should fined) __________________, and perhaps jailed, if they continue to disturb people with their **constant** calls for attention and money. E-mail was designed to be a helpful tool to allow people all over the world to communicate quickly and efficiently, but spam threatens to destroy this amazing advance in human communication.

to levy: to collect by legal authority

constant: nonstop; continuous

References

Flynn, N., & Kahn, R. (2003) *E-mail rules: A business guide to managing policies, security, and legal issues for e-mail and digital communications.* New York: American Management Association.

Freeman, J. (2009). *The tyranny of e-mail: The four-thousand-year journey to your inbox.* New York: Scribner.

Building Better Vocabulary

ACTIVITY 16 Practicing Three Kinds of Vocabulary from Context

Read each important vocabulary word or phrase. Locate it in the essay if you need help remembering the word or phrase. Then circle the best synonym, antonym, or collocation from column A, B, or C.

Type of Vocabulary	Important Vocabulary	A	B	C
Synonyms	**1.** nurture	encourage	happen	injure
	2. entire	friendly	numerous	whole
	3. a component	an essay	a part	a reason
	4. vital	necessary	personal	slow
Antonyms	**5.** shut down	deliver	start	tolerate
	6. delete	add	explain	taste
	7. constant	always	once	totally
	8. allow	flood	prohibit	waste
Collocations	**9.** a ___ employees	disaster's	company's	method's
	10. even ___	delicious	poor	worse
	11. ___ instantly	internal	private	virtually
	12. a means of ___	communication	millions	trouble

Original Student Writing: Argument Essay

In this section, you will follow the seven steps in the writing process to write an argument essay.

ACTIVITY 17 Step 1: Choose a Topic

Your first step is to choose a topic for your essay that you understand well, including both sides of the issue. Your teacher may assign a topic, you may think of one yourself, or you may choose one from the suggestions below. As you consider possible topics, ask yourself, "What do I know about this topic? What do my readers know? Even though I know this topic well, do I need additional information in order to explain the topic better to my readers?"

Humanities	Present an argument about the quality of a movie. Should your readers see the movie or not?
Sciences	Is it right to use animals to test the safety of medicines and health products for humans?
Business	Should the government eliminate the national minimum wage?
Personal	When should you disagree with your parents?

1. What topic did you choose? ____________________

2. Why did you choose this topic? ____________________

____

3. How well do you know this topic? What is your experience with it?

____

____

ACTIVITY 18 Step 2: Brainstorm

Write a thesis statement that expresses your opinion about the issue. Keep in mind that a thesis statement cannot be a question. Then jot down at least three pro ideas and three con ideas for the thesis statement.

Thesis statement: ____________________

Pro	Con
1.	1.
2.	2.
3.	3.

ACTIVITY 19 Step 3: Outline

Prepare a simple outline of your essay. This outline is for five paragraphs, but you may have more or fewer paragraphs if your teacher approves.

Title: ____________________

I. Introduction

A. Hook: ____________________

____

B. Connecting information: ____________________

____

C. Thesis statement: ____________________

____

II. Body Paragraph 1 (Supporting Point 1): ______________________________

A. ______________________________

____

B. ______________________________

____

III. Body Paragraph 2 (Supporting Point 2): ______________________________

A. ______________________________

____

B. ______________________________

____

IV. Body Paragraph 3: ______________________________

A. Concession: ______________________________

____

B. Refutation: ______________________________

____

V. Conclusion: ______________________________

____

Peer Editing of Outlines

Exchange books with a partner. Read your partner's outline. Then use the following questions to help you to comment on your partner's outline. Use your partner's feedback to revise your outline.

1. Is there any aspect of the outline that is unclear to you? Give details here.

____

____

____

2. Can you think of an area in the outline that needs more development? Make specific suggestions.

____

____

____

3. If you have any other ideas or suggestions, write them here.

___

___

___

ACTIVITY 20 Step 4: Write the First Draft

Use the information from Steps 1–3 to write the first draft of your argument essay. Use at least four of the vocabulary words or phrases from the Building Better Vocabulary activities in this unit. Underline these words and phrases in your essay.

ACTIVITY 21 Step 5: Get Feedback from a Peer

Exchange papers from Step 4 with a partner. Read your partner's first draft. Then use Peer Editing Sheet 1 on ELTNGL.com/sites/els to help you to comment on your partner's writing. Be sure to offer positive suggestions and comments that will help your partner improve his or her essay.

ACTIVITY 22 Step 6: Revise the First Draft

Read the comments from your peer editor. Then reread your essay. Can you identify places where you should make revisions? List the improvements you plan to make.

1. ___

___

___

2. ___

___

___

3. ___

___

___

Use all the information from the previous steps to write the final version of your paper. Often, writers will need to write a third or even a fourth draft to express their ideas as clearly as possible. Write as many drafts as necessary to produce a good essay.

ACTIVITY 23 Step 7: Proofread the Final Draft

Be sure to proofread your paper several times before you submit it so you find all the mistakes and correct them.

Additional Topics for Writing

Here are ten more ideas for topics for additional argument essay writing.

PHOTO TOPIC: Look at the photograph on pages 24–25. In most places, the minimum driving age is between 16 and 18, and drivers can keep their licenses as long as they are good drivers. Do you think there should be a maximum age after which a person can no longer keep a driver's license?

TOPIC 2: Should lawyers work hard to defend a client they think is guilty?

TOPIC 3: Should public libraries have filters on computers that limit the kinds of Internet sites that patrons can access?

TOPIC 4: Most countries offer free education through high school. Should university education also be free?

TOPIC 5: Should television shows be allowed to use adult language?

TOPIC 6: Should the requirements for your college major be changed?

TOPIC 7: Should women be allowed to serve in combat positions in the military?

TOPIC 8: Should parents send their children to a school that gives instruction in more than one language?

TOPIC 9: Should junk food manufacturers be allowed to advertise their products to children?

TOPIC 10: Should health care be provided by the government?

Timed Writing

How quickly can you write in English? There are many times when you must write quickly, such as on a test. It is important to feel comfortable during those times. Timed-writing practice can make you feel better about writing quickly in English.

1. Read the essay guidelines below. Then take out a piece of paper.
2. Read the writing prompt below the guidelines.
3. Write a basic outline, including the thesis and the main points of support for your argument. You should spend no more than five minutes on your outline.
4. Write a five-paragraph essay.
5. You have 40 minutes to write your essay.

Argument Essay Guidelines

- Be sure to present and refute a counterargument in the body of your essay.
- Remember to give your essay a title.
- Double-space your essay.
- Write as legibly as possible (if you are not using a computer).
- Include a short introduction (with a thesis statement), three body paragraphs, and a conclusion.
- Try to give yourself a few minutes before the end of the activity to review your work. Check for spelling and the correct use of modals and *-ly* adverbs.

Should people eat a vegetarian diet? Write an argument essay for or against vegetarianism.

NOTES

ON THE EDGE 3

A two-week-old rescued orphan elephant with her keeper in Nairobi National Park, Kenya

ACADEMIC SKILLS

READING	Understanding appositives
GRAMMAR	Using appositives
CRITICAL THINKING	Analyzing text organization
WRITING SKILL	Reviewing the thesis statement

THINK AND DISCUSS

1 What endangered species are you aware of?
2 What are some reasons these animals are endangered?

EXPLORE THE THEME

A Look at the information on these pages and answer the questions.

1. Which big cat on these pages do you think is most in danger? Why?
2. Why do you think conservationists think it is important to protect these animals?

B Match the words in blue to their definitions.

_______________ (n) animals that kill and eat other animals
_______________ (n) the animals that another animal eats for food
_______________ (n) the illegal catching and/or killing of animals
_______________ (adj) possible and practical to do or achieve
_______________ (adj) hiding your feelings or actions from others

BIG CATS IN CRISIS

Snow Leopard

The secretive snow leopard is known as the "ghost of the mountains." Its home is in the Himalayas and surrounding ranges of Central Asia.

Estimated wild population: 4,000 to 8,700

Population in zoos: 414

Status: Vulnerable

The big cats on these pages are all in danger of disappearing from the wild. A major reason is loss of habitat resulting from human population growth in the areas where they live. Additional threats are posed by illegal **poaching** for skins and other body parts, and killing by ranchers when the cats eat their livestock. Conservationists, however, believe it is still **feasible** to save these **predators**.

Lion

Lions once roamed across Africa and into Asia; today, the largest lion population is in Tanzania.

Estimated wild population: 20,000 to 30,000

Population in zoos: 1,888

Status: Vulnerable

Cheetah

The cheetah uses its incredible speed to chase down its **prey**. It is found mainly in east and southwest Africa; another 70–110 live in Iran.

Estimated wild population: 7,000 to 10,000

Population in zoos: 1,015

Status: Vulnerable

Tiger

The biggest cat, with some males weighing over 600 pounds (270 kilograms). Three tiger subspecies have gone extinct since the 1930s; four or five other subspecies survive in Asia.

Estimated wild population: Fewer than 4,000

Population in zoos: 1,660

Status: Endangered

Reading

PREPARING TO READ

BUILDING VOCABULARY

A The words in **blue** below are used in the reading passage. Match the correct form of each word to its definition.

Manatees—known as "sea cows" because of their unhurried pace—were listed as an endangered species in 1967. Since then, **dedicated** efforts by conservationists have helped bring them back from the edge. In the shallow, crowded waters of North America's Atlantic coast, collisions between manatees and fishing boats were frequent and often **lethal** to the animals. Officials therefore introduced boating speed limits near locations **assessed** to be important manatee habitats. From 1991 to 2016, the Florida manatee population climbed from 1,267 to around 6,300, a 500 percent increase. With the continued **resolve** of conservationists and local officials, experts **project** that the manatee population will continue to grow.

1. When something is ________________, it is examined or considered carefully.
2. If something is ________________, it is potentially deadly.
3. ________________ is determination to do what you have decided to do.
4. If you ________________ that something will happen, you expect it to happen.
5. If you are ________________ to something, you are committed to doing it.

A mother manatee and her baby at Three Sisters Springs, Florida, United States

B Complete the definitions with the words in the box. Use a dictionary to help you.

BUILDING VOCABULARY

acknowledge	apparently	authority	hypothetical	priority

1. A(n) ________________ on a particular subject is someone who can give expert information or advice about that subject.
2. You use the word "________________" to indicate that the information you are giving is something that you have heard, but you are not certain that it is true.
3. If you ________________ something, you accept or admit that it is true or that it exists.
4. If something is ________________, it is based on possible ideas or situations rather than actual ones.
5. If something is a(n) ________________, it is the most important thing you have to do or deal with.

C Note answers to the questions below. Then discuss with a partner.

USING VOCABULARY

1. What organizations do you know that are **dedicated** to protecting endangered animals? What do they do?

____

____

____

2. Are there any endangered animals that you think should be a **priority** for conservation efforts? Explain your answer.

____

____

____

D Skim the reading passage. What aspects of tigers do you think the author will discuss? List three ideas. Then read the article and check your predictions.

SKIMMING / PREDICTING

____

____

____

____

Reading

A CRY FOR THE TIGER

by Caroline Alexander

A lone tiger hunts in the forests of northern Sumatra, Indonesia.

We have the means to save the mightiest cat on Earth. But do we have the will?

Track 3

A **Dawn, and mist covers the forest.** Only a short stretch of red dirt track can be seen. Suddenly—emerging from the red-gold haze of dust and misted light—a tigress walks into view. First, she stops to rub her right-side whiskers against a roadside tree. Then she crosses the road and rubs her left-side whiskers. Then she turns to regard us with a look of bored indifference.

B Consider the tiger, how she is formed. The claws of a tiger are up to four inches long and retractable,[1] like those of a domestic cat; her teeth can shatter bone. While able to achieve bursts above 35 miles an hour, the tiger is a predator built for strength, not sustained speed. Short, powerful legs propel her lethal attacks. The eye of the tiger is backlit by a membrane, a thin piece of skin that reflects light through the retina—the secret of the animal's famous night vision and glowing night eyes. The roar of the tiger—*Aaaaauuuunnnn!*—can carry more than a mile.

C For weeks, I had been traveling through some of the best tiger habitats in Asia, but never before had I seen a tiger. Partly this was because of the animal's legendarily secretive nature. The tiger is powerful enough to kill and drag prey five times its weight, yet it can move through high grass, forest, and even water in unnerving silence. Those who have witnessed—or survived—an attack commonly report that the tiger "came from nowhere."

D But the other reason for the lack of sightings is that the ideal tiger landscapes have very few tigers. The tiger has been a threatened species for most of my lifetime, and its rareness has come to be regarded—like its dramatic coloring—as a defining attribute. The common view that the tiger will continue to be "rare" or "threatened" is no longer tenable.[3] In the early 21st century, tigers in the wild face complete annihilation. "This is about making decisions as if we're in an emergency room," says Tom Kaplan, co-founder of Panthera, an organization dedicated to big cats. "This is it."

E The tiger's enemies are well-known. Loss of habitat is exacerbated by exploding human populations. Poverty contributes to the poaching of prey animals. Above all, there is the dark threat of a black market for tiger parts. Less acknowledged are decades of botched conservation strategies. The tiger population, dispersed among Asia's 13 tiger countries, is estimated at fewer than 4,000 animals, though many conservationists believe there are hundreds less than that. To put this number in perspective: Global alarm for the species was first sounded in 1969, and early in the 1980s it was estimated that some 8,000 tigers remained in the wild. So decades of concern for tigers—not to mention millions of dollars donated by well-meaning individuals—has failed to prevent the loss of perhaps half of an already threatened population.

[1]If something is **retractable**, it can be moved in and out or back and forth.
[2]The **retina** is the area at the back of the eye.
[3]If an argument is **tenable**, it is reasonable and can be successfully defended against criticism.

> "If the core breeding grounds are lost, you will have tiger landscapes with no tigers."

My determination to see a wild tiger in my lifetime brought me to Ranthambore Tiger Reserve, one of 40 in India. India is home to some 50 percent of the world's wild tigers. The 2010 census reported a maximum estimate of 1,909 in the country—up 20 percent from the previous estimate. While this is welcome news, most authorities regard the new figure as reflecting better census methods rather than growth of the tiger population: Tiger counts, in India or elsewhere, are still at best only estimates. A modest 41 of these tigers were living in Ranthambore.

F

Reserves such as Ranthambore exist as islands of fragile habitat in a vast sea of humanity, yet tigers can range over a hundred miles, seeking prey, mates, and territory. An unwelcome revelation of the new census is that nearly a third of India's tigers live outside tiger reserves, a situation that is dangerous for both humans and animals. Prey and tigers can only disperse if there are recognized corridors[4] of land between protected areas to allow safe passage. No less critical, such passages would serve as genetic corridors, essential to the long-term survival of the species.

G

It is a heady[5] experience to see an idealistic map of Asia's tiger landscapes linked by these not-yet-existent corridors. A spiderweb of green lines weaves among core tiger populations, forming a network that includes breathtaking extremes of habitat—Himalayan foothills, jungle, swamp, forest, grasslands. However, close examination breaks the spell. The places that have actual tigers—here-and-now,

H

[4]**Corridors** are strips of land that connect one place to another.
[5]A **heady** experience strongly affects your senses, such as, by making you feel excited.

Tiger cubs at a water hole in Bandhavgarh National Park, India

Last Strongholds

An estimated 100,000 tigers roamed Asia a hundred years ago. Fewer than 4,000 may remain in the wild today. Most tigers survive only in protected areas in South and Southeast Asia.

Historic range

Present range

areas where tigers are most likely to breed and repopulate surrounding habitats

habitat outside of breeding areas with evidence of tigers in the past decade

national park or wildlife sanctuary; many of these no longer have tigers due to poaching

habitat where tigers could survive but are no longer found

Human population density (per sq. mi.)

3,000+

1,000–3,000

Vital corridors

Many of India's tigers live along the Western Ghats mountains, where there is evidence that tigers are finding corridors between protected areas.

flesh-and-blood tigers—as opposed to **hypothetical** ones, are represented by a scattering of brown-colored spots. The master plan is ambitious, but is it **feasible**? Over the next decade, infrastructure projects—the kind of development that often destroys habitat—are **projected** to average some $750 billion a year in Asia.

"I've never met a head of state who says, 'Look, we're a poor country, if it comes between tigers and people, you just have to write off tigers,'" said Alan Rabinowitz, an **authority** on tigers and the CEO of Panthera. "The governments don't want to lose their most majestic animal. They consider it part of what makes their country what it is, part of the cultural heritage. They won't sacrifice a lot to save it, but if they can see a way to save it, they will usually do it."

Seeing a way has proved difficult due to the variety of tiger strategies, programs, and initiatives competing for attention—and funding. Long-term conservation must focus on all aspects of a tiger landscape: core breeding populations, sanctuaries, wildlife corridors, and the surrounding human communities. In an ideal world, all would be funded; as it is, different agencies adopt different strategies for different components.

With time running out, tough **priorities** must be set. "Since the 1990s, there has been what I would sum up as mission drift," said Ullas Karanth of the Wildlife Conservation Society, who is one of the world's most respected tiger biologists. **Apparently**, the drift toward tiger conservation activities like eco-development and social programs—which possibly have greater fund-raising appeal than antipoaching patrols—

takes away funds and energy from the single most vital task: safeguarding core breeding populations of tigers. "If these are lost," Karanth said, "you will have tiger landscapes with no tigers."

Decades of experience and failures have yielded a conservation strategy that, according to Rabinowitz, "allows any site or landscape to increase its tigers if followed correctly." Central to this approach is the need for systematic patrolling and monitoring of sites **assessed** as harboring defensible core tiger populations. In this way, a population of a mere half dozen breeding females can rebound.[6]

For now, the essential task is to save the few tigers that actually exist. In November 2010—the Year of the Tiger—the world's 13 tiger countries came together at the Global Tiger Summit in St. Petersburg, Russia. Together, they agreed on the need "to double the number of wild tigers across their range by 2022." Most authorities believe that the fight to save the tiger can be won—but that it must be fought with tireless professional focus that keeps to a proven strategy. It will require the human species to display not merely **resolve** but outright zealotry.[7]

[6]If something **rebounds**, it successfully goes back to a previous state or level.

[7]If someone displays **zealotry**, they display very extreme views and behavior.

Adapted from "A Cry for the Tiger," by Caroline Alexander: National Geographic Magazine, December 2011.

Caroline Alexander is the author of several best-selling books, including *The Bounty: The True Story of the Mutiny on the Bounty* (2004), for which she was nominated for the National Book Critic's Circle Award.

A Bengal tiger in the Sundarbans, India, pauses in a river to listen to another tiger's roar.

UNDERSTANDING THE READING

A Check (✓) three statements that best summarize the writer's main ideas.

UNDERSTANDING MAIN IDEAS

☐ 1. Safeguarding main breeding areas should be a top priority for tiger conservation.

☐ 2. It is a positive sign that tigers have been spotted outside of tiger reserves in India.

☐ 3. We should not accept the idea the tiger will continue to be a rare species; it might die out completely.

☐ 4. Patrolling and monitoring core tiger areas can help to increase tiger populations.

☐ 5. The last few decades of tiger conservation strategies have generally been successful.

☐ 6. Establishing land corridors for Indian tigers is probably unrealistic as a long-term strategy.

B Match each question with the correct answer. Three items are extra.

UNDERSTANDING DETAILS

1. When did the world first realize that tigers were endangered? ________
2. How many tigers were estimated to be alive in the early 1980s? ________
3. What percentage of the world's tigers lives in India? ________
4. How many tigers are in Ranthambore? ________
5. Approximately how many tigers in India live outside of tiger reserves? ________
6. What year was the St. Petersburg Global Tiger Summit? ________
7. How many countries have natural tiger habitats? ________

a. 2010
b. 41
c. the 1990s
d. 4,000
e. 1969
f. 1/3
g. 8,000
h. 20 percent
i. 50 percent
j. 13

C Complete the chart with information from the reading.

IDENTIFYING PROBLEMS, REASONS, AND SOLUTIONS

Problem: Tigers are endangered	
Possible Reasons	**Possible Solutions**
Past conservation efforts were not effective *Growth of human populations*	

CRITICAL THINKING Writers **organize their texts** in specific ways in order to reveal certain information at specific times. Identifying and understanding the organizational structure of a text can help with reading comprehension. The organizational structure can reveal a writer's purpose and point of view. The reader can also anticipate what kind of information might be coming next.

CRITICAL THINKING: ANALYZING TEXT ORGANIZATION

D How does the writer organize the article? Number the ideas in the correct order (1–5).

_______ a. reasons for why tigers have become rare

_______ b. an outline of a variety of global initiatives to save the tiger

_______ c. a description of the power and mystery of tigers

_______ d. a detailed explanation of how one country is trying to protect tiger habitats

_______ e. a description of how urgent it is to save the last remaining tigers

CRITICAL THINKING: ANALYZING TEXT ORGANIZATION

E Discuss the questions with a partner.

1. Do you think the opening of the article is effective? Why or why not?
2. How else could the writer have organized the article?

CRITICAL THINKING: GUESSING MEANING FROM CONTEXT

F Find and underline the following words and phrases in the reading passage. Use the context to help you identify the meaning of each word or phrase. Then match each word or phrase with its definition.

1. Paragraph A: **indifference** _____
2. Paragraph C: **unnerving** _____
3. Paragraph D: **defining attribute** _____
4. Paragraph D: **annihilation** _____
5. Paragraph E: **botched** _____
6. Paragraph E: **dispersed** _____
7. Paragraph G: **unwelcome revelation** _____
8. Paragraph L: **harboring** _____

a. an unpleasant and surprising discovery
b. a key characteristic to someone's identity
c. lack of interest or concern
d. total defeat or destruction
e. spread over a wide area
f. failed; mismanaged
g. giving a safe home or shelter to (something)
h. making (someone) lose courage or confidence

CRITICAL THINKING: PERSONALIZING

G How important do you think it is to protect endangered animals? Note your ideas below. Then discuss with a partner.

____

____

____

DEVELOPING READING SKILLS

READING SKILL Understanding Appositives

An appositive is a noun or a noun phrase that explains, defines, or gives more information about another noun or noun phrase that is close to it. Writers use commas, dashes, or colons to separate appositives from the nouns that they describe. For example, the underlined phrases in the sentences below are appositives. The double-underlined words are the nouns that they describe.

"I've never met a head of state who says, 'Look, we're a poor country. If it comes between tigers and people, you just have to write off tigers,'" said Alan Rabinowitz, an authority on tigers and the CEO of Panthera.

A spiderweb of green lines weaves among core tiger populations, forming a network that includes breathtaking extremes of habitat—Himalayan foothills, jungle, swamp, forest, grasslands.

Long-term conservation must focus on all aspects of a tiger landscape: core breeding populations, sanctuaries, wildlife corridors, and the surrounding human communities.

UNDERSTANDING APPOSITIVES

A **In each of these sentences from the passage, underline the appositive and circle the noun or noun phrase that it refers to. One sentence has two noun phrase appositives that refer to two different nouns.**

1. My determination to see a wild tiger in my lifetime brought me to Ranthambore Tiger Reserve, one of 40 in India.
2. "This is about making decisions as if we're in an emergency room," says Tom Kaplan, co-founder of Panthera, an organization dedicated to big cats.
3. The places that have actual tigers—here-and-now, flesh-and-blood tigers—as opposed to hypothetical ones, are represented by a scattering of brown-colored spots.
4. Over the next decade, infrastructure projects—the kind of development that often destroys habitat—are projected to average some $750 billion a year in Asia.
5. In November 2010—the Year of the Tiger—the world's 13 tiger countries came together at the Global Tiger Summit in St. Petersburg, Russia.

Video

A pair of Siberian tiger cubs

TIGERS IN THE SNOW

BEFORE VIEWING

DISCUSSION

A What threats to tigers do you remember from the reading? Make a list.

____

____

LEARNING ABOUT THE TOPIC

B Read the information. Then answer the questions.

Siberian (or Amur) tigers live mainly in the forests of Russia's far east, though some still exist in China and North Korea. The climates that these tigers live in are harsh—temperatures in some areas can drop to –40°C—but this also offers some advantages. These cold northern forests offer the lowest human density of any tiger habitat, allowing the tigers far more room to move around. However, the Siberian tiger, like other tiger species, is endangered. Estimates suggest that there are fewer than 500 individuals left in Russia.

1. In what kind of areas do Siberian tigers live? What advantages do these areas offer the tigers?

   ____

   ____

2. Why do you think Siberian tigers might be endangered?

   ____

C Read these extracts from the video. Match the correct form of each **bold** word to its definition.

VOCABULARY IN CONTEXT

"Once the kill has been made, it's clear the male is the **dominant** partner. He won't allow the female to get near until he's had enough."

"They are at the top of their **food chain**, but the tigers are still endangered."

"It is thought its fragile population has been **stabilized** for the moment."

1. ______________ (v) to get to a state in which there aren't any more big problems or changes
2. ______________ (adj) more powerful, successful, influential, or noticeable than others
3. ______________ (n) the process by which one living thing is eaten by another, which is then eaten by another, and so on

WHILE VIEWING

A ▶ Watch the video. Check the main idea.

UNDERSTANDING MAIN IDEAS

- ☐ a. Siberian tigers are in danger, but their populations are currently remaining steady.
- ☐ b. Siberian tigers are in danger, and their populations are decreasing very quickly.
- ☐ c. Siberian tigers were endangered, but their populations are now getting bigger.

B ▶ Watch the video again. Then answer the questions below.

UNDERSTANDING DETAILS

1. How is a Siberian tiger different from other tigers?

   ____

2. How big does a Siberian tiger's territory have to be?

   Female: ______________ Male: ______________

3. According to the video, what are the two main threats to Siberian tigers?

   ____

4. How has the Siberian tiger's decline changed since the mid-1990s?

   ____

AFTER VIEWING

A Why do you think male tigers need such a large home range? Note your ideas below. Then discuss with a partner.

CRITICAL THINKING: MAKING INFERENCES

____

B How does the Siberian tiger's situation compare with the challenges facing other tigers? Note your ideas below. Then discuss with a partner.

CRITICAL THINKING: SYNTHESIZING

____

____

Writing

EXPLORING WRITTEN ENGLISH

VOCABULARY FOR WRITING

A The following words and expressions can be useful when writing about problems and solutions. Use the words to complete the definitions.

threatened (paragraph D)	**exacerbated** (paragraph E)	**sacrifice** (paragraph I)
initiatives (paragraph J)	**funding** (paragraph J)	**components** (paragraph J)
safeguarding (paragraph K)	**strategy** (paragraph L)	

1. ______________ is money that a government or organization provides for a particular purpose.
2. If an animal species is ______________, it is likely to become endangered.
3. ______________ are parts or elements of a larger whole.
4. If something ______________ a problem or bad situation, it made it worse.
5. ______________ are important actions that are intended to solve a particular problem.
6. ______________ something is keeping it from harm or danger.
7. A(n) ______________ is a plan of action designed to achieve a long-term or overall aim.
8. If you ______________ something that is valuable or important, you give it up, usually to obtain something else for yourself or for other people.

A critically endangered female Sumatran tiger and her five-month-old cub

B Read the information in the box. Then use appositives to combine the sentence pairs (1–5).

LANGUAGE FOR WRITING Using Appositives

As you saw in the Reading Skill section, writers use appositives to give more information about a noun. Appositives help writers avoid redundancy and short, choppy sentences. You can separate appositives with commas, dashes, or colons.

With an appositive:
"I've never met a head of state who says, 'Look, we're a poor country. If it comes between tigers and people, you just have to write off tigers,'" said Alan Rabinowitz, a renowned authority on tigers and the CEO of Panthera.

Without an appositive:
"I've never met a head of state who says, 'Look, we're a poor country. If it comes between tigers and people, you just have to write off tigers,'" said Alan Rabinowitz. Rabinowitz is a renowned authority on tigers and the CEO of Panthera.

1. The Bengal tiger is one of India's most popular attractions. The Bengal tiger is India's national animal.

   ____

   ____

2. In addition to tigers, other animals live in Ranthambore. Monkeys, deer, wild boars, owls, and parakeets live in Ranthambore.

   ____

   ____

3. Ranthambore is home to 41 tigers. Ranthambore is a former private hunting estate.

   ____

   ____

4. Fateh Singh Rathore used to work at Ranthambore when it was a hunting estate. Fateh Singh Rathore is the assistant field director of the reserve.

   ____

   ____

5. Zaw Win Khaing once saw a tiger in 2002. Zaw Win Khaing is the head ranger of a tiger reserve in Myanmar.

   ____

   ____

WRITING SKILL Reviewing the Thesis Statement

Individual paragraphs have main ideas. Similarly, essays have main ideas. A **thesis statement** is a statement that expresses the main idea of an entire essay. A good thesis statement has the following characteristics:

- It presents your position or opinion on the topic.
- It includes a reference to the reasons for your opinion or position on the topic.
- It expresses only the ideas that you can easily explain in your body paragraphs.

CRITICAL THINKING: EVALUATING

C **Read the following pairs of thesis statements. Check (✓) the statement in each pair that you think is better. Then share your answers with a partner.**

1. a. ☐ Palisades Park should be protected for three main reasons: It is the only park in the city, it is a gathering place for families, and it is a safe place for children to play after school.

   b. ☐ Palisades Park is a beautiful place for parents to spend time with their children and for people in the community to gather for events.

2. a. ☐ The Bloodroot plant (*Sanguinaria Canadensis*) is endangered and should be protected because it can cure dozens of ailments, from skin disorders to cancer.

   b. ☐ The Bloodroot plant (*Sanguinaria Canadensis*), an endangered plant found in the forests of North America, can be used to cure diseases.

A bloodroot plant

CRITICAL THINKING: EVALUATING

D **Read the question below about tiger conservation. Write your opinion and two reasons. Then use your opinion and your reasons to write a thesis statement.**

Should governments spend more money to protect tigers?

My opinion: ____

____

Reason 1: ____

____

Reason 2: ____

____

Thesis statement: ____

____

____

REVISING PRACTICE

The draft below is an opinion essay about protecting nature. Follow the steps to create a better second draft.

1. Add the sentences (a–c) in the most suitable spaces.
   a. With a combination of international and local efforts, Borneo may be saved from destruction.
   b. so that we can save all the different forms of life that live on the island.
   c. because it is home to so many different species and because the rain forest helps reverse damage from climate change.
2. Now fix the following problems (a–c) with the essay.
   a. Cross out one sentence that doesn't relate to the topic of the essay in paragraph B.
   b. Use an appositive to revise the first two sentences in paragraph C.
   c. Use an appositive to revise sentences five and six in paragraph D.

A

The rain forest island of Borneo, the world's third largest island, is about the size of the state of Texas in the United States. The island is one of the most biodiverse places in the world. It is home to endangered animals such as the Sumatran tiger, the Sumatran rhinoceros, the pygmy elephant, and the Bornean orangutan. And nearly 400 new species have been discovered in 10 years. Sadly, this island's diverse and beautiful rain forest is in danger. In the past 20 years, 80 percent of the rain forest has been destroyed because of illegal logging, forest fires, and development. At the same time, people are capturing and selling some of the wildlife, particularly the orangutans. We need to protect Borneo ________________

B

It's important to protect Borneo ________________. Visitors to Borneo can enjoy its beautiful beaches and mountains. Thousands of species of plants, animals, and insects live on Borneo. Many, like the pygmy elephant, cannot be found anywhere else on Earth. In addition, scientists continue to find new species of plants and animals. Some of these might provide medicines for diseases or teach us more about biology.

C

We also need to protect Borneo in order to protect the globe from climate change. Borneo is home of one of the world's remaining rain forests. Carbon dioxide, a greenhouse gas, is heating up Earth's atmosphere and causing a number of problems such as extreme weather and melting polar ice. Rain forests absorb carbon dioxide and create more oxygen. They also help produce rain all around the world. If we lose rain forests, we will lose one of our best weapons against global warming.

D

So, what can be done to protect Borneo? Both international and local communities are involved in saving the island. An organization called the World Wildlife Fund (WWF) is working to create safety corridors and protect the 220,000-square-kilometer (85,000-square-mile) area from destruction. The organization is raising funds to help make this happen. The Borneo Project is an international organization. The Borneo Project provides support to local communities. These communities protect the rain forests of Borneo in various ways: They stop loggers from cutting down trees, they educate the local community about the need to save the rain forest, and they block developers from building on the land. ______________

Orangutans in a Borneo forest sanctuary

EDITING PRACTICE

Read the information below. Then find and correct one mistake with appositives in each of the sentences (1–5).

In sentences with appositives, remember that an appositive must:

- be a noun or a noun phrase.
- come right after a noun or noun phrase.
- be separated by commas, dashes, or colons.

1. Tigers, they are an endangered species, live throughout Asia.
2. Ranthambore, a tiger reserve is in India.
3. Tiger conservationists—people who protect tigers, are looking for new solutions.
4. Corridors, are paths for safe travel, may help tigers survive in wild areas.
5. There are fewer than 4,000 tigers. The biggest cat in the world.

UNIT REVIEW

Answer the following questions.

1. What are two reasons tigers are endangered?

____

____

2. What are two ways we can help protect tigers?

____

____

3. What are two things a thesis statement should include?

____

____

4. Do you remember the meanings of these words? Check (✓) the ones you know. Look back at the unit and review the ones you don't know.

☐ acknowledge AWL	☐ poaching
☐ apparently AWL	☐ predator
☐ assess AWL	☐ prey
☐ authority AWL	☐ priority AWL
☐ dedicated	☐ project AWL
☐ feasible	☐ resolve AWL
☐ hypothetical AWL	☐ secretive
☐ lethal	

NOTES

SURVIVAL INSTINCT 4

According to Yellowstone National Park, the chances of a park visitor being injured by a grizzly bear are 1 in 2.7 million.

ACADEMIC SKILLS

READING Identifying adverbial phrases
CRITICAL THINKING Interpreting figurative language

THINK AND DISCUSS

1 Do you know of anyone who has experienced a dangerous situation? What happened?
2 What kind of people do you think are most likely to survive dangerous situations?

EXPLORE THE THEME

A Look at the information on these pages and answer the questions.

1. What makes K2 difficult to climb?
2. What do you think is significant about the Pakistani side of the mountain?
3. Why do you think K2 is called the "savage mountain"?

B Match the correct form of the words in blue to their definitions.

____________________ (n) a trip made for a specific purpose

____________________ (n) a surface that is at an angle

____________________ (n) the top of a mountain

THE SAVAGE MOUNTAIN

K2 is unique in high-altitude mountaineering. Although shorter than Mount Everest (Mount Qomolangma) by about 240 meters, it has long been known as "the mountaineer's mountain." Its distinctive shape—a towering, triangular silhouette with steep **slopes**—makes it the classic image of a mountain. But it also makes K2 one of the most difficult and dangerous to climb.

By 2010, Everest had been climbed more than 5,000 times; in contrast, K2 had been successfully climbed just over 300 times. For every four climbers who've succeeded, one K2 climber has died. Charles Houston and Robert Bates titled the account of their failed 1953 **expedition** *K2: The Savage Mountain.* A year later, K2 was finally "conquered" by an Italian expedition that put two men on the top via the Pakistani side of the mountain.

The diagram on these pages shows the route taken by the 2011 K2 North Pillar Expedition. Most attempts to reach the **summit** of K2 come from the Pakistani side; the approach via the north side is even more challenging, and rarely attempted.

K2 North Glacier

N

To Advanced Base Camp
Altitude 4,650 m

SUMMIT
8,611 meters (28,251 ft)
Japanese Couloir
Bivouac site
8,300 m
August 22
CAMP IV
7,950 m
August 21
Tent site
7,900 m
CAMP III
7,250 m
August 20
Tent site
7,300 m
CAMP II
6,600 m
August 19
Shoulder Depot Camp
6,250 m
August 18
Middle Camp
5,950 m
North Ridge
Northwest Ridge
CAMP I
5,300 m
Summit push: August 16-17

Reading 1

PREPARING TO READ

BUILDING VOCABULARY

A **The words in blue below are used in Reading 1. Read the paragraphs about a climbing expedition. Then match the correct form of each word to its definition.**

On November 8, 2014, three climbers set out to reach the summit of one of the highest peaks in Southeast Asia: Myanmar's Hkakabo Razi. To travel as lightly as possible on their final day, they left their food and **gear** behind at their camp. It was a decision that would determine the **fate** of the expedition.

Their final **task** was to complete the last few kilometers to the summit. But after four hours of climbing, they were still not close enough. Climber Cory Richards still **recalls** his **sensation** of fear as the team neared the peak: "I think we should turn around now." If the team carried on, he realized, they would have to spend a **terrifying** night on the mountain with no tents, sleeping bags, or food. The team agreed to end its expedition and to **descend** Hkakabo Razi the next day.

Climber Renan Ozturk feels they made the right choice: "The decision is, do you want to push hard enough to lose your toes, your fingers, or your life? That's always the trick with Himalayan climbing. You have to be good enough to know [when] to turn around."

1. ________________ (v) to go down
2. ________________ (v) to remember
3. ________________ (n) a feeling or emotional state
4. ________________ (adj) extremely frightening
5. ________________ (n) an assignment; a job to be performed
6. ________________ (n) equipment; usually used with outdoor activities
7. ________________ (n) a result or an outcome that is beyond your control

USING VOCABULARY

B **Discuss these questions with a partner.**

1. What aspect of climbing a high-altitude mountain might be most **terrifying**?
2. What **gear** would be needed for climbing a mountain like Hkakabo Razi or K2?

SKIMMING

C **Skim the reading passage. What kind of reading is it? Discuss your idea with a partner. Then check your answer as you read.**

a. a work of fiction   b. a scientific article   c. a true story

The expedition members climb a steep edge of K2's North Ridge.

DEADLY SUMMIT

Track 4

A During the summer of 2011, a team of climbers attempted to climb the world's second highest peak—K2. Their goal was to climb the North Ridge on the Chinese side of the mountain without bottled oxygen or high-altitude porters.[1]

B The team included two Kazakh climbers, an Argentinian photographer, and a videographer from Poland. All four had attempted K2 climbs before, but none had yet reached the peak. The fifth member, Gerlinde Kaltenbrunner, was a 40-year-old former nurse from Austria. If she succeeded, she would be the first woman in history to climb all of the world's tallest peaks without supplemental oxygen. Gerlinde was leading the **expedition** with her husband, Ralf Dujmovits, 49, who had previously reached the **summit** of K2 from the Pakistani side.

C Starting on July 5, the six climbers established a series of camps, connected by thousands of feet of rope. These would give the expedition members places to rest during their ascent. To establish the route, they had to cope with vertical rock walls, avalanches,[2] and **slopes** covered in chest-deep snow.

D On August 16, the team started the actual climb to the summit. Two days later, at around 6:30 a.m., Ralf stopped. The snow conditions were becoming dangerous, and he could no longer ignore his gut instinct.[3] "Gerlinde, I am going back," he said.

E On their first climb together, Gerlinde and Ralf had made an agreement: neither would stand in the other's way if one wanted to continue and the other did not. Gerlinde had never been to the top of K2, so she was willing to take risks that Ralf was not. She coped with fear differently, too. Ralf liked

[1]A **porter** is someone who helps carry your bags or equipment.

[2]An **avalanche** is a mass of snow, ice, and rocks that falls down a mountainside.

[3]**Gut instinct** is a feeling you have that you can't explain logically.

how the sensation of fear in his stomach acted as a warning, compelling him to pay attention. Gerlinde strove to block out fear with a quiet calm. If she kept herself completely focused on the task at hand,[4] she didn't feel scared.

F But now Ralf begged his wife to come down with him. "Ralf was yelling that the route is very, very avalanche prone. He was shouting desperately," recalled Maxut Zhumayev, one of the Kazakh climbers. "Gerlinde shouted in return that now is the moment when the fate of the climb will be decided." She was concerned that if they turned around now, they would miss the period of good weather.

G "I was really afraid I would never see her again," Ralf explained later.

H Gerlinde watched as Ralf descended into the mist. Then she focused on the task ahead. "It's not that I was indifferent to the risk," she said afterward. "But my gut feeling was good."

I As Ralf had feared, the snow was becoming loose. Later that day, a small avalanche hit Tommy Heinrich, the Argentinian, who was climbing below the others; it knocked him upside down and stuffed[5] his nose and mouth. Only the fixed rope kept him from being swept off the mountain. He eventually dug himself out, but decided that he, too, would turn back.

J So now they were four: Gerlinde, Maxut and Vassiliy (the two Kazakh climbers), and the videographer, Dariusz. The team spent a miserable night crammed into a two-person tent. Two days later, on August 20, they reached Camp III, exhausted and chilled to the bone. They drank coffee with honey and warmed their hands and feet over their gas stoves. All night the frosted tent walls snapped in the wind.

K The weather improved on Sunday, August 21, helping to carry the team to Camp IV. They were now at nearly 8,000 meters, in the so-called death zone. Here the body struggles to deal with the oxygen-thin air. Cognition is affected, and even simple tasks seem to take forever. The team checked their gear and melted snow for water. Below them, a terrifying void[6] plunged nearly two miles to the glacier below. Two thousand feet above was the glistening white summit.

L "There was a moment when we all started to get nervous, in a good way," Gerlinde said later. "We touched each other's hands and looked at each other in the eyes and said, 'OK, tomorrow is our day.'"

M On August 22, they were greeted by a cloudless day, the weather like a gift. The gales were gone, and the sky ran blue and cloudless. But with only a third of the oxygen at sea level, snow up to their chests in places, and stinging blasts of icy wind, the climbers made painfully slow progress. By 1 p.m., they had gained less than 180 meters.

N From Advanced Base Camp, Ralf guided them by phone and watched as their figures, no bigger than commas on a piece of paper, edged toward the peak. After climbing for 12 hours, they were just 300 meters below the summit. On the radio, Ralf urged Gerlinde to return to Camp IV for the night now that they had broken the trail and knew the way.

O "You cannot sleep there, you cannot relax," he said.

P "Ralf," said Gerlinde, "we are here. We don't want to go back."

Q With the sun low in the west, the team stopped to put up a tiny tent on the edge of a crevasse.[7] After an hour of hacking at the ice, they had a platform four feet wide. They secured the tent with ice axes, and by 8:15 they were sitting inside, a stove hanging from the ceiling with a pot of melting snow. The temperature was minus 25 Celsius. They would rest until morning, then resume the push for the prize, now so close.

[4]If something is **at hand**, it is in front of you or is the thing you are now dealing with.

[5]To **stuff** something is to fill or block it up.

[6]A **void** is an empty space.

[7]A **crevasse** is a deep crack, especially in ice or a snow-covered mountain.

They set out around 7 a.m. as another clear morning dawned. By mid-afternoon, they reached the base of a ramp beneath the summit ridge. For the first 20 meters, the snow only covered their shins. But soon the snow became chest deep. "Oh no," Gerlinde thought, "it's not possible that we've come so far up and will have to turn back…" With a surge of energy and hope, she finally crawled out of the ramp and onto the ridge. It was 4:35 p.m. She could see the summit dome.

"You can make it!" Ralf cried over the radio. "You can make it! But you are late! Take care!"

She sipped from her water bottle. Her throat was cracked; it hurt to swallow. It was too cold to sweat, and she was dehydrated just from panting for air.

And then she walked the final steps to the apex of K2, reaching the summit at 6:18 p.m.

She wanted to share the moment with Ralf, but when she opened the radio, she couldn't speak. There were mountains in every direction. Mountains she had climbed. Mountains that had stolen the lives of friends and nearly claimed hers, too. Alone, with the world at her feet, she turned from one point of the compass to another.

Fifteen minutes later, Maxut and Vassiliy arrived, shoulder to shoulder, followed by Dariusz. Everyone embraced. It was 7 p.m. Dariusz filmed Gerlinde as she tried to explain what it meant to be there at that moment. She began to cry, then composed herself. "It was very, very hard, … and now it's just amazing." She gestured to the sea of peaks in all directions, as a golden light began to burnish[8] the world. "You see all this—I think everybody can understand why we do this."

[8] When you **burnish** something, such as metal, you rub it or polish it to make it shiny.

Members of the 2011 K2 expedition team take their final steps toward the summit.

UNDERSTANDING THE READING

SUMMARIZING

A **Complete the summary of the reading passage. Write no more than two words in each space.**

In the summer of [1] ______________, a team of mountain climbers attempted to climb [2] ______________. The team consisted of [3] ______________ climbers, including one woman, Gerlinde Kaltenbrunner. First, they set up a number of [4] ______________ along a ridge on the north side of the mountain. Then they began their ascent. The climb soon became dangerous, and [5] ______________ climbers eventually decided to turn back, including Gerlinde's [6] ______________, Ralf Dujmovits. After a few days, the [7] ______________ improved, allowing the climbers to reach an altitude known as the [8] ______________. They pushed on and finally reached the summit on August 23. Gerlinde became the [9] ______________ to climb all of the world's highest peaks without using extra [10] ______________.

UNDERSTANDING MAIN IDEAS

B **How did the climbers respond to fear during the climb? Check (✓) four statements that best summarize the information in paragraphs D–H.**

☐ 1. Gerlinde and Ralf reacted differently to their fears.

☐ 2. Most of the climbers were concerned and wanted to turn back.

☐ 3. Ralf felt fear and knew he should return to base camp.

☐ 4. Gerlinde blocked out her fear and focused on climbing.

☐ 5. Ralf was keen that the other team members continue.

☐ 6. Gerlinde was prepared to take risks that Ralf would not.

SEQUENCING

C **Put the events (a–h) of the climb in order on the timeline.**

a. The team members get to Camp III.
b. The team members enter the "death zone."
c. The team starts the climb to the summit.
d. The weather turns bad, and Ralf quits the climb.
e. The team begins setting up camps along the route.
f. The team members get within 300 meters of the summit.
g. Gerlinde and other team members reach the summit.
h. An avalanche hits Tommy Heinrich, and he decides to drop out.

July 5 ☐ — Aug 16 ☐ — Aug 18 ☐ — ☐ — Aug 20 ☐ — ☐ — ☐ — Aug 23 ☐

D Find and underline the following words in **bold** in the reading passage. Use context to identify their meanings. Then match each word to its definition.

INFERRING MEANING

_____ 1. **supplemental** (paragraph B)
_____ 2. **indifferent** (paragraph H)
_____ 3. **crammed** (paragraph J)
_____ 4. **plunged** (paragraph K)
_____ 5. **apex** (paragraph U)

a. sloped downward at a steep angle
b. the top or summit
c. additional
d. not feeling concerned
e. put in with too many other people or things in a space that is too small

CRITICAL THINKING If a sentence or phrase doesn't make sense literally, it might be an example of **figurative language**. For example, in paragraph E, Gerlinde and Ralf agreed not to "stand in each other's way." This means that they agreed not to stop each other from doing what they wanted. You can look for clues in the context of a sentence to help you understand the meaning of figurative language.

E Think about the meaning of the underlined parts of these excerpts. Then discuss your answers to the questions with a partner.

CRITICAL THINKING: INTERPRETING FIGURATIVE LANGUAGE

1. "On August 22, they were greeted by a cloudless day, the weather <u>like a gift</u>."

   Why did the good weather feel like a gift to the climbers?

   ____

   ____

2. "Ralf guided them by phone and watched as their figures, <u>no bigger than commas on a piece of paper</u>, edged toward the peak."

   Why does the writer compare the human figures with commas on paper?

   ____

   ____

3. "<u>Mountains that had stolen the lives of friends</u> and nearly claimed hers, too."

   What happened to some of Gerlinde's friends? How might this have affected her feelings toward these mountains?

   ____

   ____

F Look back at Gerlinde's quote in the final paragraph. Do you think the reward that mountaineers get is worth the risk? Why or why not?

CRITICAL THINKING: REFLECTING

I don't think the risk is worth it because . . .

I think it's worth the risk. Mountain climbing . . .

DEVELOPING READING SKILLS

READING SKILL Identifying Adverbial Phrases

Adverbs (e.g., *quickly*, *today*) give more information about an action or event, such as *when, why, where,* or *how* something happens. An **adverbial phrase** is a group of words that acts like an adverb. It can modify verbs, adjectives, adverbs, clauses, and even entire sentences. However, it is different from a clause because it does not contain a subject and a verb.

Reason (why):

The team stopped to put up a tiny tent.

Note: The infinitive phrase is used as an adverbial phrase instead of an object of the verb in this example. To differentiate between the two uses, replace the infinitive phrase with *in order to*. An infinitive phrase functioning as an adverbial can be replaced with *in order to*.

The team stopped in order to put up a tiny tent. (adverbial phrase)

The team decided to put up a tent. (object)

Manner (how):

They secured the tent with ice axes.

Time (when):

By 8:15, they were sitting inside . . .

IDENTIFYING ADVERBIAL PHRASES

A Underline the adverbial phrases in these excerpts from the reading passage.

1. During the summer of 2011, a team of climbers attempted to climb the world's second highest peak. ____________
2. Their goal was to climb the North Ridge on the Chinese side of the mountain. ____________
3. To establish the route, they had to cope with vertical rock walls, avalanches, . . . ____________
4. If she succeeded, she would be the first woman in history to climb all of the world's tallest peaks without supplemental oxygen. ____________
5. On their first climb together, Gerlinde and Ralf had made an agreement. ____________
6. Below them, a terrifying void plunged to the glacier below. ____________
7. But . . . the climbers made painfully slow progress. ____________
8. They would rest until morning, then resume the push for the prize. ____________
9. With a surge of energy and hope, she finally crawled onto the ridge. ____________
10. Fifteen minutes later, Maxut and Vassiliy arrived, . . . ____________

IDENTIFYING ADVERBIAL PHRASES

B Look at each adverbial phrase that you underlined in exercise A. Identify the purpose of each phrase. Write *when, why, where,* or *how* on the lines.

APPLYING

C Find three more examples of adverbial phrases in the reading passage and note the kinds of information they provide.

Video

Although shark attacks can be dangerous, they rarely occur.

SURVIVAL LESSONS

BEFORE VIEWING

A What do you think you should do in these situations? Discuss your ideas with a partner. PREDICTING

1. If a shark attacks you, you should ________________.
   a. splash violently   b. attack its eyes   c. pretend to be dead
2. If an elephant is charging toward you, you should ________________.
   a. run between its legs   b. turn and run   c. scream and yell

B Read the information below. Then answer the questions with a partner. LEARNING ABOUT THE TOPIC

Animal	Number of People Killed (annually)
mosquitoes	725,000
snakes	50,000
crocodiles	1,000
elephants	500
deer	120
bees	53
sharks	10

1. Why do you think mosquitoes kill so many more people than sharks?

   ____

2. Which of these animals are you most worried about? Why?

   ____

VOCABULARY IN CONTEXT

C Below are some quotes from the video. Match each **bold** phrase to its definition.

"The probability of getting killed is much lower if you **stand your ground** than if you run."

"[…] if he really wants to, he can **catch up** to you, and you don't want to run away."

"A limp body tells the shark it's time to **tuck in** for a big meal."

1. ________________ (v) to eat and enjoy
2. ________________ (v) to stay where you are and refuse to move
3. ________________ (v) to move faster in order to reach someone or something

WHILE VIEWING

UNDERSTANDING MAIN IDEAS

A ▶ Watch the video. What is the main idea?

a. that sharks and elephants are usually scared of people
b. how to survive if you encounter shark and elephant attacks
c. that shark and elephant attacks are becoming less common

UNDERSTANDING DETAILS

B ▶ Watch the video again. For each statement, circle T for true or F for false.

1. Most species of shark are man-eaters.	**T**	**F**
2. Sharks usually bite because they are hungry.	**T**	**F**
3. A shark may swim away if you hit its gills.	**T**	**F**
4. Elephants show their ears to give a warning.	**T**	**F**
5. You should not show your back to an elephant.	**T**	**F**
6. Elephants can run faster than humans.	**T**	**F**

AFTER VIEWING

REACTING TO THE VIDEO

A Look back at your answers to exercise A in Before Viewing. Did you choose the same options as the advice in the video? Did you find the answers surprising? Discuss with a partner.

____

____

REFLECTING

B Do you know any other survival tips for encounters with wild animals? Discuss with a partner.

____

____

Reading 2

PREPARING TO READ

A The words and phrases in blue below are used in Reading 2. Complete each sentence with the correct word or phrase. Use a dictionary to help you.

BUILDING VOCABULARY

alter	assume	consciously	crisis	demonstrate
determination	instantly	separate	take over	version

1. A ______________ of something is one form of it.
2. When you ______________ something, you change it.
3. A ______________ is a very serious or dangerous situation.
4. When you ______________ a situation, you gain control of it.
5. If something happens ______________, it happens immediately.
6. If you ______________ two things, you keep them away from each other.
7. When you ______________ how something works, you show how it works.
8. If you do something ______________, you notice or realize that you are doing it.
9. If you ______________ something, you believe it is true based on available facts.
10. If you have ______________ to do something, you will not let anything stop you.

B Discuss these questions with a partner.

USING VOCABULARY

1. What kinds of jobs do you think require a lot of **determination**?
2. What characteristics can help a person deal well with a **crisis**?
3. What kinds of experiences can **alter** a person's life?

C When you feel scared, what do you do to calm down? Note your answers and discuss with a partner.

BRAINSTORMING

____

____

D Skim the reading passage. What do you think it will be about? Complete the statement below. Then check your idea as you read.

PREDICTING

I think the reading will be about ______________________ and about a woman who ______________________________.

As part of their military training, Indian Army soldiers practice yoga to help them deal with stress.

BREATH OF LIFE

Track 5

A When we encounter a stressful or frightening situation, our heart rate increases, our breath quickens, and our muscles become tense—these all happen naturally. In fact, for most of history, we have assumed that there is a line separating our natural, basic instinct and our learned behavior. But recent brain research has proved that our brain can change in structure and function throughout our life, depending on our experiences. So would it be possible to train our brain to control our "natural responses," such as to fear?

B One of the most surprising ways to control our fear response is breathing. Combat trainers, for example, use "tactical breathing" techniques to prepare FBI agents for crisis situations. These are basically the same concepts taught in yoga classes. One version that police officers learn works like this: Breathe in for four counts; hold for four counts; breathe out for four counts; hold for four; start again. How could something so simple be so powerful?

C The breath is one of the few actions that reside in both our somatic nervous system (which we can consciously control) and our autonomic system (which includes our heartbeat and other actions we cannot easily access). So the breath is a bridge between the two. By consciously slowing down the breath, we can slow down the primal fear response that otherwise takes over.

D One scientific study demonstrated how rhythmic breathing can actually alter the brain. Sara Lazar, an instructor at Harvard Medical School, scanned the brains of 20 people who meditate for 40 minutes a day. When she compared their brain images with those of nonmeditating people of similar ages and backgrounds, she found a significant difference. The meditators had 5 percent thicker brain tissue in the parts of the brain that are used during meditation—that is, the parts that handle emotion regulation, attention, and working memory, all of which help control stress.

E Studies such as those conducted at Harvard suggest that meditators—like deep-breathing police officers—may have found a way for us to evolve past the basic human fear response. With training, it may be possible to become better prepared for a life-or-death situation.

A SURVIVOR'S STORY

F In January 2000, photographer Alison Wright, 45, was riding a bus in Laos when it was struck by a logging truck. According to medical professionals, she should have died that day. Wright's determination to live—combined with her ability to regulate her fear response—enabled her to defy the odds.

G "When the truck hit, I slammed my head hard. I know it sounds cliché,[1] but all I could see was a bright white light—I had to ask myself if I'd died. The impact instantly broke my back [and] ribs; my left arm plunged through the window and was shredded to the bone; ... my diaphragm[2] and lungs were punctured; my heart, stomach, and intestines tore loose and actually lodged in my shoulder.

H When I came to,[3] I looked around the bus, which was on its side, and the endorphins[4] kicked in. I pushed apart the seats that pinned me down and managed to pull myself out of the bus and crawl out onto the road. Then I realized how difficult it was to breathe, and I started to think about my situation in very matter-of-fact terms. Like, I remember not wanting to cry and waste any water with my tears, and I checked to make sure I had my wallet so that if I died, people could ID me.

[1]If an idea or a phrase is **cliché**, it has been used so much that it is no longer interesting.

[2]Your **diaphragm** is a muscle between your lungs and stomach that is used for breathing.

[3]When you **come to**, you regain consciousness.

[4]**Endorphins** are chemicals that occur naturally in the brain and that can block the feeling of pain.

"I knew that if I was going to survive, I had to calm myself down and get my breathing under control."

I knew that if I was going to survive, I had to calm myself down and get my breathing under control. I'd studied meditation and yoga for years, both of which focus on breathing techniques. I was able to call on that experience to calm my breathing and, as a result, calm myself. I remember looking at the bamboo moving in the wind around me, and waiting for help, just focusing on my breaths.

I I was eventually rescued that day by a passing aid worker, who drove me seven hours to a hospital. Back home in San Francisco, though, I faced new challenges. Physically, I had to totally rebuild my muscles, which had atrophied[5] after four months in bed. Doctors told me I should accept the fact that my life would never be the same. Obviously, they didn't know me. When one told me I'd never have abdominal muscles[6] again, I worked toward doing sit-ups. I eventually did a thousand a day. Every morning I'd wake up and put my feet on the ground and feel gratitude.

J

I set the goal of climbing Mount Kilimanjaro, which I did in 2004. For years, I suffered from post-traumatic stress disorder[7] and had horrible nightmares about the accident. But in 2005, I traveled back to Laos and rode the same bus route again. I realized then what a gift it was to be thrown into adversity[8] and come out on the other end. ”

K

[5]If a part of the body has **atrophied,** it has weakened because of disease, bad nutrition, or injury.

[6]**Abdominal muscles** are the muscles in the stomach area.

[7]**Post-traumatic stress disorder**, or PTSD, is a psychological condition that can occur after a frightening or stressful experience.

[8]**Adversity** is a very difficult situation.

POSTSCRIPT

L

Following her rehabilitation, Alison Wright recorded her experiences in her memoir, *Learning to Breathe: One Woman's Journey of Spirit and Survival.* Wright's accident inspired her to set up a charity—the Faces of Hope Fund—that aims to "give back in some small way to the communities" that she photographs. Her first activity as the founder of Faces of Hope was to return with five doctors and $10,000 worth of medical supplies to the village and people in Laos that saved her life.

Wright visiting an earthquake victim in Haiti in 2010

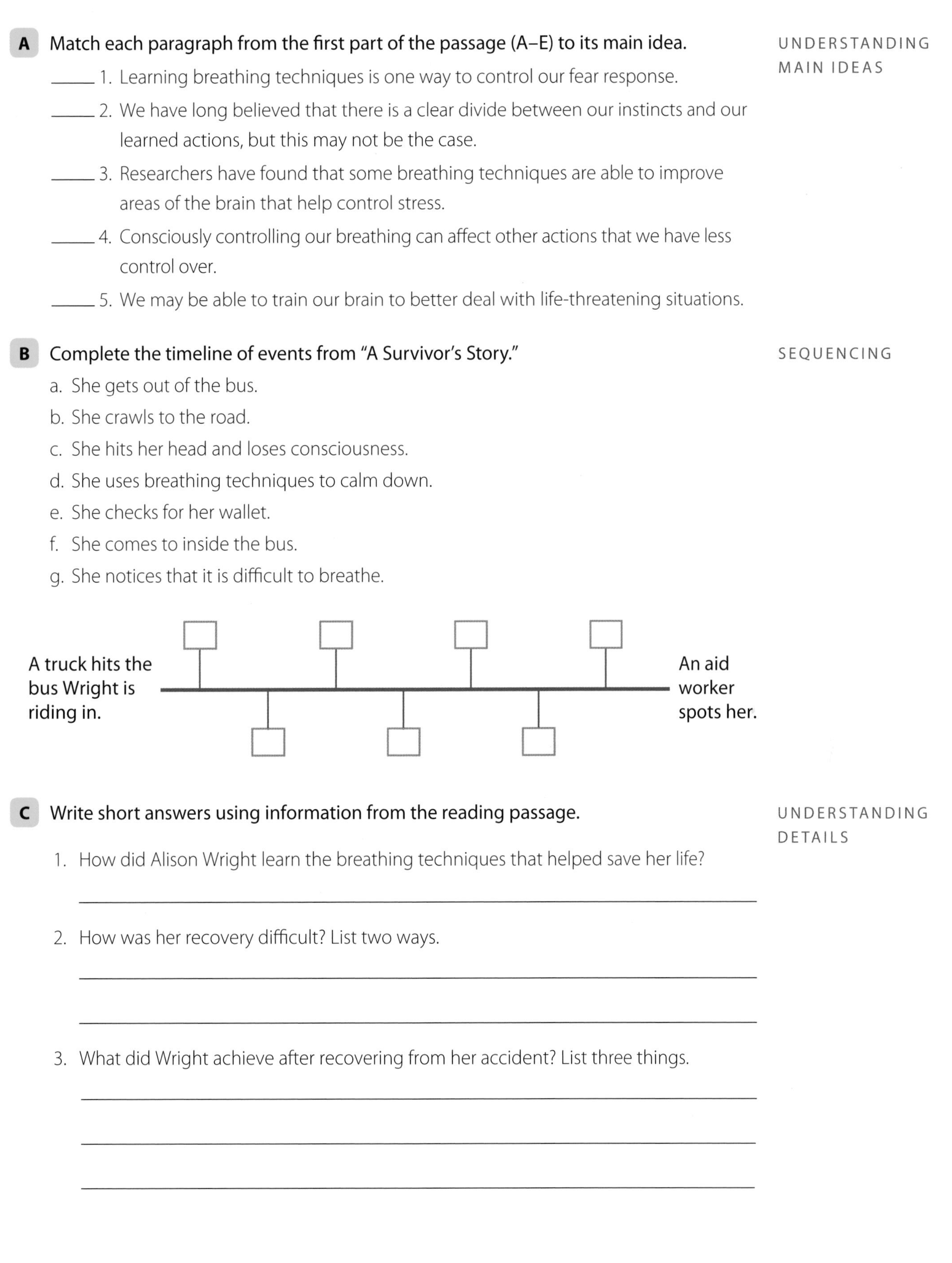

UNDERSTANDING THE READING

A Match each paragraph from the first part of the passage (A–E) to its main idea.

UNDERSTANDING MAIN IDEAS

_____ 1. Learning breathing techniques is one way to control our fear response.

_____ 2. We have long believed that there is a clear divide between our instincts and our learned actions, but this may not be the case.

_____ 3. Researchers have found that some breathing techniques are able to improve areas of the brain that help control stress.

_____ 4. Consciously controlling our breathing can affect other actions that we have less control over.

_____ 5. We may be able to train our brain to better deal with life-threatening situations.

B Complete the timeline of events from "A Survivor's Story."

SEQUENCING

a. She gets out of the bus.
b. She crawls to the road.
c. She hits her head and loses consciousness.
d. She uses breathing techniques to calm down.
e. She checks for her wallet.
f. She comes to inside the bus.
g. She notices that it is difficult to breathe.

C Write short answers using information from the reading passage.

UNDERSTANDING DETAILS

1. How did Alison Wright learn the breathing techniques that helped save her life?

____

2. How was her recovery difficult? List two ways.

____

____

3. What did Wright achieve after recovering from her accident? List three things.

____

____

____

CRITICAL THINKING: APPLYING IDEAS

D **Which ideas from paragraphs A–E does Alison Wright's story illustrate? Check (✓) the two best answers.**

☐ 1. People who meditate 40 minutes a day may have better memories than people who do not meditate.

☐ 2. Using yoga breathing techniques can help people control their fear response.

☐ 3. Rhythmic breathing can change the features of the brain.

☐ 4. Rhythmic breathing can help people control stress.

☐ 5. Breathing is part of both the somatic and autonomic systems.

IDENTIFYING ADVERBIAL PHRASES

E **For each sentence below, underline the adverbial phrase and write *when*, *how*, or *why*.**

1. ____________ Combat trainers, for example, use "tactical breathing" techniques to prepare FBI agents for crisis situations.
2. ____________ By consciously slowing down the breath, we can slow down the primal fear response that otherwise takes over.
3. ____________ With training, it may be possible to become better prepared for a life-or-death situation.
4. ____________ I was able to call on that experience to calm my breathing and, as a result, calm myself.
5. ____________ Every morning I'd wake up and put my feet on the ground and feel gratitude.

CRITICAL THINKING: INTERPRETING FIGURATIVE LANGUAGE

F **Read the quote by Alison Wright. Note your answers to the questions. Then discuss them with a partner.**

"I realized then what a gift it was to be thrown into adversity and come out on the other end."

1. What does Alison Wright mean by being "thrown into adversity"? What does it mean to "come out on the other end"?

____

____

2. In what ways do you think she might feel her experience was "a gift"?

____

____

CRITICAL THINKING: SYNTHESIZING

G **How were Gerlinde Kaltenbrunner's and Alison Wright's responses to fear similar? Note two ideas. Then discuss with a partner.**

____

____

UNIT REVIEW

Answer the following questions.

1. Whose personal experience in this unit did you find the most interesting? Why?

    ____

    ____

    ____

2. How is an adverbial phrase different from a clause?

    ____

    ____

    ____

3. Do you remember the meanings of these words? Check (✓) the ones you know. Look back at the unit and review the ones you don't know.

Reading 1:

☐ descend ☐ expedition ☐ fate
☐ gear ☐ recall ☐ sensation
☐ slope ☐ summit ☐ task AWL
☐ terrifying

Reading 2:

☐ alter AWL ☐ assume AWL ☐ consciously
☐ crisis ☐ demonstrate AWL ☐ determination
☐ instantly ☐ separate ☐ take over
☐ version AWL

VOCABULARY EXTENSION UNIT 1

WORD PARTNERS Expressions with *cut*

Many expressions with *cut* can be used in business settings. For example, you can use *cut back* to talk about reducing the number of employees or the amount of waste. Below are some other expressions with *cut*.

cut across: to affect many similar businesses, industries, or groups

cut through: to solve or deal with a problem quickly

a cut above: a product that is better than another similar product

cut one's losses: to stop losing money by getting out of a business situation

cut corners: to produce a product quickly or cheaply (often with bad results)

cut one's teeth on: to learn something useful at the start of a process or career

Complete each sentence with the correct word from the box below. One word is extra.

across	back	corners	losses	teeth	through

1. During the recession, many companies cut ______________ on hiring new employees.
2. After a large number of complaints about the product, the company decided to cut its ______________ and stop producing any more of it.
3. Environmental problems often cut ______________ many cities and countries.
4. Young sales representatives can cut their ______________ on becoming familiar with products and customers. They then have the skills to become successful managers.
5. Some businesses want to cut ______________ regulations that they think are preventing them from growing faster.

VOCABULARY EXTENSION UNIT 3

WORD PARTNERS Adjective/Verb + *priority*

Here are some adjectives that collocate with the noun *priority*.

high *priority*
low *priority*
first */* ***top*** */* ***number one*** *priority*
urgent */* ***immediate*** *priority*

Below are some verbs that also collocate with *priority*. Read the definitions.

If you ***give priority*** *to something, you make it the most important thing.*
If you ***identify priorities****, you decide on the most important things to do.*
If one thing ***takes priority*** *over another, it's more important.*

A Circle the best option to complete each sentence.

1. Many parents tell their children that doing homework should **identify** / **take** priority over playing video games.
2. For most businesses, customer satisfaction is a **high** / **low** priority.
3. When boarding a plane, airlines often **give** / **take** priority to families with young children.
4. Before a hurricane strikes, evacuating residents in the hurricane's path is the **first** / **high** priority.
5. Compared to math and science, the teaching of arts is a **first** / **low** priority for many publicly-funded schools.
6. To manage your workload, **give** / **identify** priorities that are urgent versus ones that are less important.
7. As a parent, my **number one** / **low** priority in life is taking care of my son.

B Complete the sentences about yourself.

1. My number one priority in life is ______________________________

   ______________________________.
2. For me, ______________________________

   takes priority over ______________________________.
3. Next week, ______________________________
   is an urgent priority.

VOCABULARY EXTENSION UNIT 4

WORD FORMS Adjectives Ending in *-ed* and *-ing*

Adjectives that end in *-ed* often describe someone's feelings, e.g., *scared*. Adjectives that end in *-ing* describe the characteristic of a person, thing, or situation. For example, something that is *terrifying* makes someone feel *terrified*. Below are more examples of adjectives that can end in *-ed* or *-ing*.

confused—confusing	*irritated—irritating*	*tired—tiring*
relaxed—relaxing	*shocked—shocking*	*surprised—surprising*

Circle the correct adjectives to complete the paragraph.

My most [1] **terrified** / **terrifying** experience was when I went trekking with my friends. Our map app didn't work because there was no cell phone service. This made me [2] **irritated** / **irritating** because I thought the phone would work fine. The signs along the trekking path were [3] **confused** / **confusing**, so we ended up getting lost. We were also [4] **shocked** / **shocking** to discover that we had forgotten our water bottles. Fortunately, we found a stream and drank some water. This made us feel [5] **relaxed** / **relaxing** again. Then my friend spotted a path near the stream. We were all relieved when the path took us back to our car.

WRITING REFERENCE

UNIT 1

Language for Writing: Using Adjective Clauses

Adjective clauses (also known as relative clauses) give more information about subject and object nouns in the main clauses of sentences. An adjective clause contains a subject, a verb, and a relative pronoun. The adjective clause functions in a similar way to an adjective—it gives descriptive information about a noun.

> *One resource* ***that is disappearing*** *is fresh water.*
>
> *The author* ***who wrote the article*** *has strong feelings.*
>
> *The Leonardo DiCaprio Foundation works on issues* ***that concern our planet****, such as climate change and wildlife conservation.*

We use different relative pronouns to introduce different kinds of information.

Relative pronoun	Used for ...
that	people, things
which	things
who	people
whose	someone's belongings

Restrictive and Nonrestrictive Adjective Clauses

Restrictive adjective clauses give essential information about the noun. Do not use commas with restrictive adjective clauses.

> *I read an article* ***that*** *didn't really change my mind.*
>
> *I read the article* ***that*** *you told me about.*

Nonrestrictive adjective clauses give extra, or nonessential, information about the noun. Commas always set off nonrestrictive adjective clauses.

> *Petroleum,* ***which*** *is a nonrenewable resource, is getting harder to extract.*
>
> *The author,* ***who*** *is a noted environmentalist, gave a lecture at the university.*

Brief Writer's Handbook

Understanding the Writing Process: The Seven Steps

The Assignment

Imagine that you have been given the following assignment: *Write an essay in which you discuss one aspect of vegetarianism.* What should you do first? What should you do second, third, and so on? There are many ways to write, but most good writers follow certain steps in the writing process. These steps are guidelines that are not always followed in order.

Look at this list of steps. Which ones do you regularly do? Which ones have you never done?

STEP 1: Choose a topic.

STEP 2: Brainstorm.

STEP 3: Outline.

STEP 4: Write the first draft.

STEP 5: Get feedback from a peer.

STEP 6: Revise the first draft.

STEP 7: Proofread the final draft.

Next, you will see how one student, Hamda, went through the steps to do the assignment. First, read the final essay that Hamda gave her teacher.

Essay 1

Better Living as a Vegetarian

1 The hamburger has become a worldwide cultural icon. Eating meat, especially beef, is an integral part of many diverse cultures. Studies show, however, that the consumption of large quantities of meat is a major contributing factor toward a great many deaths, including the unnecessarily high number of deaths from heart-related problems. Although it has caught on slowly in Western society, vegetarianism is a way of life that can help improve not only the quality of people's lives but also their longevity.

2 Surprising as it may sound, vegetarianism can have beneficial effects on the environment. Because demand for meat animals is so high, cattle are being raised in areas where rain forests once stood. As rain forest land is cleared in order to make room for cattle ranches, the environmental balance is upset; this imbalance could have serious consequences for humans. The article "Deforestation: The hidden cause of global warming" by Daniel Howden explains that much of the current global warming is due to depletion of the rain forests.

3 More important at an individual level is the question of how eating meat affects a person's health. Meat, unlike vegetables, can contain very large amounts of fat. Eating this fat has been connected—in some research cases—to certain kinds of cancer. In fact, *The St. Petersburg*

Times reports, "There was a statistically significant risk for . . . gastric cancer associated with consumption of all meat, red meat and processed meat" (Rao, 2006). If people cut down on the amounts of meat they ate, they would automatically be lowering their risks of disease. Furthermore, eating animal fat can lead to obesity, and obesity can cause numerous health problems. For example, obesity can cause people to slow down and their heart to have to work harder. This results in high blood pressure. Meat is also high in cholesterol, and this only adds to health problems. With so much fat consumption worldwide, it is no wonder that heart disease is a leading killer.

4 If people followed vegetarian diets, they would not only be healthier but also live longer. Eating certain kinds of vegetables, such as broccoli, brussels sprouts, and cauliflower, has been shown to reduce the chance of contracting colon cancer later in life. Vegetables do not contain the "bad" fats that meat does. Vegetables do not contain cholesterol, either. Furthermore, native inhabitants of areas of the world where people eat more vegetables than meat, notably certain areas of Central Asia, routinely live to be over one hundred.

5 Some people argue that, human nature being what it is, it is unhealthy for humans to not eat meat. These same individuals say that humans are naturally carnivores and cannot help wanting to consume a juicy piece of red meat. However, anthropologists have shown that early humans ate meat only when other foods were not abundant. Man is inherently a herbivore, not a carnivore.

6 Numerous scientific studies have shown the benefits of vegetarianism for people in general. There is a common thread for those people who switch from eating meat to consuming only vegetable products. Although the change of diet is difficult at first, most never regret their decision to become a vegetarian. They feel better, and those around them comment that they look better than ever before. As more and more people are becoming aware of the risks associated with meat consumption, they too will make the change.

Steps in the Writing Process

Step 1: Choose a Topic

For this assignment, the topic was given: Write an essay on vegetarianism. As you consider the assignment topic, you have to think about what kind of essay you may want to write. Will you list different types of vegetarian diets? Will you talk about the history of vegetarianism? Will you argue that vegetarianism is or is not better than eating animal products?

Hamda chose to write an argumentative essay about vegetarianism to try to convince readers of its benefits. The instructor had explained that this essay was to be serious in nature and have facts to back up the claims made.

Step 2: Brainstorm

The next step for Hamda was to brainstorm.

In this step, you write every idea about your topic that pops into your head. Some of these ideas will be good, and some will be bad; write them all. The main purpose of brainstorming is to write as many ideas as you can think of. If one idea looks especially good, you might circle that idea or put a check next to it. If you write an idea and you know right away that you are not going to use it, you can cross it out.

Brainstorming methods include making lists, clustering similar ideas, or diagramming your thoughts.

Look at Hamda's brainstorming diagram on the topic of vegetarianism.

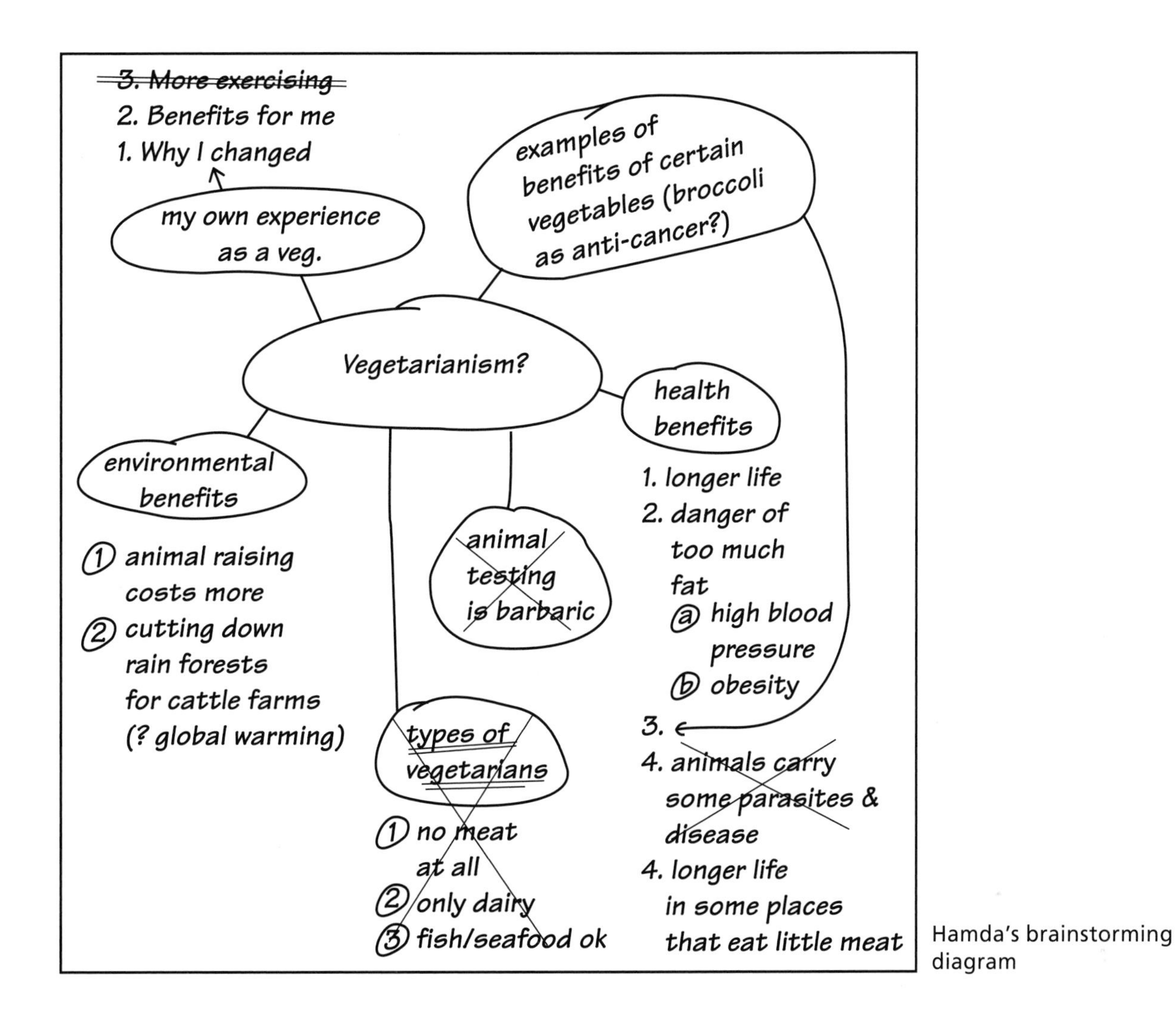

Hamda's brainstorming diagram

As you can see from the brainstorming diagram, Hamda considered many aspects of vegetarianism. Notice a few items in the diagram. As she organized her brainstorming, Hamda wrote "examples of benefits of certain vegetables" as a spoke on the wheel. Then she realized that this point would be a good number three in the list of health benefits, so she drew an arrow to show that she should move it there. Since one of Hamda's brainstorming ideas (types of vegetarians) seemed to lack supporting details and was not related to her other notes, she crossed it out.

Getting the Information

How would you get the information for this brainstorming exercise?

- You might read a book or an article about vegetarianism.
- You could spend time searching online for articles on the subject.
- You could write a short questionnaire to give to classmates asking them about their personal knowledge of vegetarian practices.
- You could also interview an expert on the topic, such as a nutritionist.

Writer's Note

Doing Research

To get a deeper understanding of your essay topic, you may choose to do some research. Remember that any information you get from an outside source needs to be credited in your essay. Writers do NOT use others' ideas in their writing without giving the proper credit.

Take another look at Hamda's essay. Can you find the places where she used outside sources to back up her ideas?

Step 3: Outline

Next, create an outline for the essay. Here is Hamda's rough outline that she wrote from her brainstorming notes.

I. Introduction
   A. Define vegetarianism
   B. List different types
   C. Thesis statement

II. Environmental benefits (Find sources to support!)
   A. Rain forests
   B. Global warming

III. Health issues (Find sources to support!)
   A. Too much fat from meat → obesity → diseases → cancer
   B. High blood pressure and heart disease
   C. Cancer-fighting properties of broccoli and cauliflower, etc.

IV. Counterargument and refutation
   A. Counterargument: Man is carnivore.
   B. Refutation

V. Conclusion
   A. Restate thesis
   B. Opinion: Life will improve.

Supporting Details

After you have chosen the main points for your essay you will need to develop some supporting details. You should include examples, reasons, explanations, definitions, or personal experiences. In some cases, such as this argumentative essay on vegetarianism, it is a good idea to include outside sources or expert opinions that back up your claims.

One common technique for generating supporting details is to ask specific questions about the topic, for example:

SUPPORT

What is it?

What happened?

How did this happen?

What is it like or not like? Why?

Step 4: Write the First Draft

Next, Hamda wrote her first draft. As she wrote each paragraph of the essay, she paid careful attention to the language she used. She chose a formal sentence structure including a variety of sentence types. In addition, her sentences varied in length, with the average sentence containing almost 20 words. (Sentences in conversation tend to be very short; sentences in academic writing tend to be longer.) Hamda also took great care in choosing appropriate vocabulary. In addition to specific terminology, such as *obesity, blood pressure,* and *consumption*, she avoided the conversational *you* in the essay, instead referring to *people* and *individuals.*

In this step, you use information from your brainstorming session and outline to write the essay. This first draft may contain many errors, such as misspellings, incomplete ideas, and comma errors. At this point, you should not worry about correcting the errors. The main thing is to put your ideas into sentences.

You may feel that you do not know what you think about the topic yet. In this case, it may be difficult for you to write, but it is important to just write, no matter what comes out. Sometimes writing helps you think, and as soon as you form a new thought, you can write it.

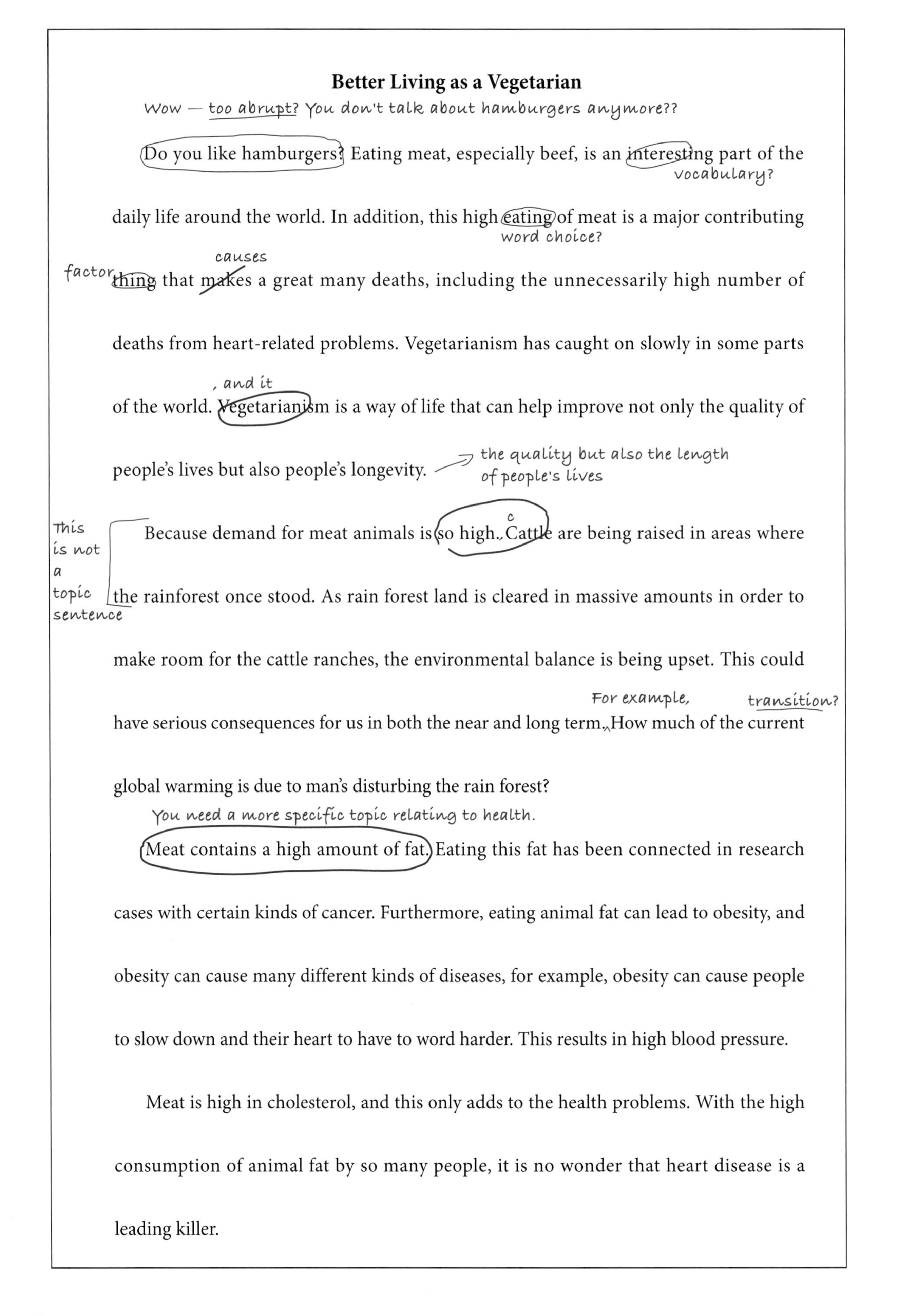

Better Living as a Vegetarian

Do you like hamburgers? Eating meat, especially beef, is an interesting part of the daily life around the world. In addition, this high eating of meat is a major contributing thing that makes a great many deaths, including the unnecessarily high number of deaths from heart-related problems. Vegetarianism has caught on slowly in some parts of the world. Vegetarianism is a way of life that can help improve not only the quality of people's lives but also people's longevity.

Because demand for meat animals is so high. Cattle are being raised in areas where the rainforest once stood. As rain forest land is cleared in massive amounts in order to make room for the cattle ranches, the environmental balance is being upset. This could have serious consequences for us in both the near and long term. How much of the current global warming is due to man's disturbing the rain forest?

Meat contains a high amount of fat. Eating this fat has been connected in research cases with certain kinds of cancer. Furthermore, eating animal fat can lead to obesity, and obesity can cause many different kinds of diseases, for example, obesity can cause people to slow down and their heart to have to word harder. This results in high blood pressure.

Meat is high in cholesterol, and this only adds to the health problems. With the high consumption of animal fat by so many people, it is no wonder that heart disease is a leading killer.

On the other hand, eating a vegetarian diet can improve a person's health. And

necessary?

vegetables taste so good. In fact, it can even save someone's life. Eating certain kinds of vegetables, such as broccoli, brussels sprouts, and cauliflower, has been shown to reduce the chance of having colon cancer later in life. Vegetables do not contain the "bad" fats that meat does. Vegetables do not contain cholesterol, either. Native inhabitants of areas of the world where mostly vegetables are consumed, notably certain areas of the former Soviet republics, routinely live to be over one hundred.

combine sentences?

good sentence

Although numerous scientific studies have shown the benefits of vegetarianism for people in general, I know firsthand how my life has improved since I decided to give up meat entirely. In 2006, I saw a TV program that discussed problems connected to animals that are raised for food. The program showed how millions of chickens are raised in dirty, crowded conditions until they are killed. The program also talked about how diseases can be spread from cow or pig to humans due to unsanitary conditions. Shortly after I saw this show, I decided to try life without eating meat. Although it was difficult at first, I have never regretted my decision to become a vegetarian. I feel better and my friends tell me that I look better than ever before.

not related to your topic

Being a vegetarian has many benefits. Try it.

This is too short! How about making a prediction or suggestion for the reader? The previous paragraph told how the writer became a vegetarian, so doesn't it make sense for the conclusion to say something like "I'm sure your life will be better too if you become a vegetarian"?

I like this essay. You really need to work on the conclusion.

Making Changes

As you write the first draft, you may want to add information or take some out. In some cases, your first draft may not follow your outline exactly. That is OK. Writers do not always stick with their original plan or follow the steps in the writing process in order. Sometimes they go back and forth between steps. The writing process is much more like a cycle than a line.

Reread Hamda's first draft with her teacher's comments.

First Draft Tips

Here are some things to remember about the first draft copy:

- The first draft is not the final copy. Even native speakers who are good writers do not write an essay only one time. They rewrite as many times as necessary until the essay is the best that it can be.
- It is OK for you to make notes on your drafts; you can circle words, draw connecting lines, cross out words, or write new information. Make notes to yourself about what to change, what to add, or what to reconsider.
- If you cannot think of a word or an idea as you write, leave a blank space or circle. Then go back and fill in the space later. If you write a word that you know is not the right one, circle or underline it so you can fill in the right word later. Do not stop writing. When people read your draft, they can see these areas you are having trouble with and offer comments that may help.
- Do not be afraid to throw some sentences away if they do not sound right. Just as a good housekeeper throws away unnecessary things from the house, a good writer throws out unnecessary or wrong words or sentences.

The handwriting in the first draft is usually not neat. Sometimes it is so messy that only the writer can read it! Use a word-processing program, if possible, to make writing and revising easier.

Step 5: Get Feedback from a Peer

Hamda used Peer Editing Sheet 8 to get feedback on her essay draft. Peer editing is important in the writing process. You do not always see your own mistakes or places where information is missing because you are too close to the essay that you created. Ask someone to read your draft and give you feedback about your writing. Choose someone that you trust and feel comfortable with. While some people feel uneasy about peer editing, the result is almost always a better essay. Remember to be polite when you edit another student's paper.

Step 6: Revise the First Draft

This step consists of three parts:

1. React to the comments on the peer editing sheet.
2. Reread the essay and make changes.
3. Rewrite the essay one more time.

Step 7: Proofread the Final Draft

Most of the hard work is over now. In this step, the writer pretends to be a brand-new reader who has never seen the essay before. Proofread your essay for grammar, punctuation, and spelling errors and to see if the sentences flow smoothly.

Read Hamda's final paper again on pages 103–104.

Of course, the very last step is to turn the paper in to your teacher and hope that you get a good grade!

Writer's Note

Proofreading

One good way to proofread your essay is to set it aside for several hours or a day or two. The next time you read your essay, your head will be clearer and you will be more likely to see any problems. In fact, you will read the composition as another person would.

Editing Your Writing

While you must be comfortable writing quickly, you also need to be comfortable with improving your work. Writing an assignment is never a one-step process. For even the most gifted writers, it is often a multiple-step process. When you were completing your assignments in this book, you probably made some changes to your work to make it better. However, you may not have fixed all of the errors. The paper that you turned in to your teacher is called a first draft, which is sometimes referred to as a rough draft.

A first draft can often be improved. One way to improve an essay is to ask a classmate, friend, or teacher to read it and make suggestions. Your reader may discover that one of your paragraphs is missing a topic sentence, that you have made grammar mistakes, or that your essay needs better vocabulary choices. You may not always like or agree with the comments from a reader, but being open to changes will make you a better writer.

This section will help you become more familiar with how to identify and correct errors in your writing.

Step 1

Below is a student's first draft for a timed writing. The writing prompt for this assignment was "For most people, quitting a job is a very difficult decision. Why do people quit their jobs?" As you read the first draft, look for areas that need improvement and write your comments. For example, does the writer use the correct verb tenses? Is the punctuation correct? Is the vocabulary suitable for the intended audience? Does the essay have an appropriate hook?

There Are Many Reasons Why People Quit Their Jobs

Joann quit her high-paying job last week. She had had enough of her coworkers' abuse. Every day they would make fun of her and talk about her behind her back. Joann's work environment was too stressful, so she quit. Many employees quit their jobs. In fact, there are numerous reasons for this phenomenon.

First, the job does not fit the worker. Job seekers may accept a job without considering their skills. Is especially true when the economy is slowing and jobs are hard to find. The workers may try their best to change themselves depending on the work. However, at some point they realize that they are not cut out in this line of work and end up quitting. This lack of understanding or ability make people feel uncomfortable in their jobs. So they begin to look for other work.

Another reason people quit their jobs is the money. Why do people work in the first place? They work in order to make money. If employees are underpaid, he cannot earn enough to support himself or his family. The notion of working, earning a decent salary, and enjoy life is no longer possible. In this case, low-paid workers have no choice but to quit their jobs and search for a better-paying position.

Perhaps the biggest situation that leads people to quit their jobs is personality conflicts. It is really difficult for an employee to wake up every morning, knowing that they will be spending the next eight or nine hours in a dysfunctional environment. The problem can be with bosses or coworkers but the result is the same. Imagine working for a discriminate boss or colleagues which spread rumors. The stress levels increases until that employee cannot stand the idea of going to work. The employee quits his or her job in the hope of finding a more calm atmosphere somewhere else.

Work should not be a form of punishment. For those people who have problems with not feeling comfortable on the job, not getting paid enough, and not respected, it *does* feel like punishment. As a result, they quit and continue their search for a job that will give them a sense of pride, safety, and friends.

Step 2

Read the teacher's comments on the first draft of "There Are Many Reasons Why People Quit Their Jobs." Are these the same things that you noticed?

The title should NOT be a complete sentence.

There Are Many Reasons Why People Quit Their Jobs

Consider changing your hook/introduction. The introduction here is already explaining one of the reasons for quitting a job. This information should be in the body of the essay. Suggestion: Use a "historical" hook describing how people were more connected to their jobs in the past than they are now.

Joann quit her high-paying job last week. She had had enough of her coworkers' abuse. Every day they would make fun of her and talk about her behind her back. Joann's work environment was too stressful, so she quit. Many employees quit their jobs. In fact, there are numerous reasons for this phenomenon.

Try to use another transition phrase instead of first, second, etc.

add transition

First, the job does not fit the worker. ^ Job seekers may accept a job without considering their

word choice—be more specific   fragment

skills. Is especially true when the economy is slowing and jobs are hard to find. The workers may

word choice—better: "adapt to"

try their best to change themselves depending on the work. However, at some point they realize

prep

that they are not cut out in this line of work and end up quitting. This lack of understanding or

S-V agreement   fragment

ability make people feel uncomfortable in their jobs. So they begin to look for other work.

word choice—be more specific

Another reason people quit their jobs is the money. Why do people work in the first place?

They work in order to make money. If employees are underpaid, he cannot earn enough to

pronoun agreement

// not parallel—use "-ing"

support himself or his family. The notion of working, earning a decent salary, and enjoy life is

word choice   Do you mean "underpaid"?

no longer possible. In this case, low-paid workers have no choice but to quit their jobs and

search for a better-paying position.

word choice—too vague

Perhaps the (biggest) situation that leads people to quit their jobs is personality conflicts. It is

word choice—avoid using "really" pronoun agreement

(really) difficult for an employee to wake up every morning, knowing that (they) will be spending

add another descriptive word here word choice—too vague

the next eight or nine hours in a dysfunctional ^ environment. The (problem) can be with bosses

punc. (add comma) word choice

or coworkers but the result is the same. Imagine working for a (discriminate) boss or colleagues

word form S-V agreement write it out—better: "can no longer"

(which) spread rumors. The stress levels (increases) until that employee (can't) stand the idea of

add transition word choice—better: "serene"

going to work. ^ The employee quits his or her job in the hope of finding a more (calm) atmosphere

somewhere else.

thought of as word choice

Work should not be ^ a form of punishment. For those people who (have problems) with not

// not parallel—use "-ing"

feeling comfortable on the job, not getting paid enough, and (not respected,) it *does* feel like

punishment. As a result, they quit and continue their search for a job that will give them a

word choice—better: "camaraderie"

sense of pride, safety, and (friends.)

Step 3

Now read the second draft of this essay. How is it the same as the first draft? How is it different? Did the writer fix all the sentence mistakes?

Two Weeks' Notice

A generation ago, it was common for workers to stay at their place of employment for years and years. When it was time for these employees to retire, companies would offer a generous pension package and, sometimes, a token of appreciation, such as a watch, keychain, or other trinket. Oh, how times have changed. Nowadays, people—especially younger workers—jump from job to job like bees fly from flower to flower to pollinate. Some observers might say that today's workforce is not as serious as yesterday's. This is too simple an explanation, however. In today's society, fueled by globalization, recession, and other challenges, people quit their jobs for a number of valid reasons.

One reason for quitting a job is that the job does not fit the worker. In other words, job seekers may accept a job without considering their aptitude for it. This is especially true when the economy is slowing and jobs are hard to find. The workers may try their best to adapt themselves to the work. However, at some point they realize that they are not cut out for this line of work and end up quitting. This lack of understanding or ability makes people feel uncomfortable in their jobs, so they begin to look for other work.

Another reason people quit their jobs is the salary. Why do people work in the first place? They work in order to make money. If employees are underpaid, they cannot earn enough to support themselves or their families. The notion of working, earning a decent salary, and enjoying life is no longer viable. In this case, underpaid workers have no choice but to quit their jobs and search for a better-paying position.

Perhaps the most discouraging situation that leads people to quit their jobs is personality conflicts. It is extremely difficult for an employee to wake up every morning knowing that he or she will be spending the next eight or nine hours in a dysfunctional and often destructive environment. The discord can be with bosses or coworkers, but the result is the same. Imagine working for a bigoted boss or colleagues who spread rumors. The stress levels increase until that employee can no longer stand the idea of going to work. In the end, the employee quits his or her job with the hope of finding a more serene atmosphere somewhere else.

Work should not be thought of as a form of punishment. For those people who struggle with not feeling comfortable on the job, not getting paid enough, and not being respected, it *does* feel like punishment. As a result, they quit and continue their search for a job that will give them a sense of pride, safety, and camaraderie.

Sentence Types

English sentence structure includes three basic types of sentences: simple, compound, and complex. These labels indicate how the information in a sentence is organized, not how difficult the content is.

Simple Sentences

1. Simple sentences usually contain one subject and one verb.

S V
Kids love television.

V S V
Does this sound like a normal routine?

2. Sometimes simple sentences can contain more than one subject or verb.

S V
Brazil and the United States are large countries.

S V V
Brazil lies in South America and has a large population.

S V V
We traveled throughout Brazil and ended our trip in Argentina.

Compound Sentences

Compound sentences are usually made up of two simple sentences (independent clauses). Compound sentences need a coordinating conjunction (connector) to combine the two sentences. The coordinating conjunctions include:

for and nor but or yet so

Many writers remember these conjunctions with the acronym *FANBOYS.* Each letter represents one conjunction: *F = for, A = and, N = nor, B = but, O = or, Y = yet,* and *S = so.*

Remember that a comma is always used before a coordinating conjunction that separates the two independent clauses.

for Meagan studied hard, **for** she wanted to pass the test.

and Meagan studied hard, **and** her classmates studied, too.

nor Meagan did not study hard, **nor** did she pass the test.

but Meagan studied hard, **but** her brother did not study at all.

or Meagan studied hard, **or** she would have failed the test.

yet Meagan studied hard, **yet** she was not happy with her grade.

so Meagan studied hard, **so** the test was easy for her.

ACTIVITY 1

Study the following examples of compound sentences. Draw a box around each subject, underline each verb, and circle each coordinating conjunction.

1. Brazil was colonized by Europeans, and its culture has been greatly influenced by this fact.
2. This was my first visit to the international section of the airport, and nothing was familiar.
3. Many people today are overweight, and being overweight has been connected to some kinds of cancer.
4. Barriers fell, markets opened, and people rejoiced in the streets because they anticipated a new life full of opportunities and freedom to make their own choices.
5. Should public school students make their own individual decisions about clothing, or should all students wear uniforms?
6. This question has been asked many times, but people are not in agreement about the ultimate punishment.

Complex Sentences

Like compound sentences, complex sentences are made up of two parts. Complex sentences, however, contain one independent clause and, at least, one dependent clause. In most complex sentences, the dependent clause is an adverb clause.

Complex Sentences (with Adverb Clauses)

Adverb clauses begin with subordinating conjunctions, which include the following:

while   although   after   because   if   before

Study the examples below. The adverb clauses are underlined, and the subordinating conjunctions are boldfaced.

The hurricane struck **while** we were at the mall.

After the president gave his speech, he answered most of the reporters' questions.

Unlike coordinating conjunctions, which join two independent clauses but are not part of either clause, subordinating conjunctions are actually part of the dependent clause.

Joe played tennis	**after** Vicky watched TV.
independent clause	dependent clause

The subordinating conjunction *after* does not connect the clauses *Joe played tennis* and *Vicky watched TV*; *after is* grammatically part of *Vicky watched TV.*

Remember that dependent clauses must be attached to an independent clause. They cannot stand alone as a sentence. If they are not attached to another sentence, they are called fragments, or incomplete sentences. Fragments are incomplete ideas, and they cause confusion for the reader. In a complex sentence, both clauses are needed to make a complete idea so the reader can understand what you mean. Look at these examples:

Fragment: After Vicky watched TV

Complete Sentence: Joe played tennis after Vicky watched TV.

or

Complete Sentence: After Vicky watched TV, she went to bed.

ACTIVITY 2

Study the following examples of complex sentences from the essays in this book. Draw a box around each subject, underline each verb, and circle each subordinating conjunction.

1. While the Northeast is experiencing snowstorms, cities like Miami, Florida, can have temperatures over 80 degrees Fahrenheit.
2. Although Brazil and the United States are unique countries, there are remarkable similarities in their size, ethnic diversity, and personal values.
3. Another bus arrived at the terminal, and the passengers stepped off carrying all sorts of luggage.
4. While it is true that everyone makes a blunder from time to time, some people do not have the courage to admit their errors because they fear blame.
5. Because almost every area has a community college, students who opt to go to a community college first can continue to be near their families for two more years.

Additional Grammar Activities

The three example essays in this section feature different grammatical errors. Each paragraph highlights one kind of error. In each case, read the entire essay before you complete the activities.

Before you complete Activities 1–5, read the whole essay first. Then go back and complete each activity.

ACTIVITY 1 Verb Forms

Read the paragraph and decide whether the five underlined verbs are correct. If not, draw a line through the verb and write the correct form above the verb.

Essay 2

A Simple Recipe

1 "When in Rome, do as the Romans do" may sound ridiculous, but this proverb offer an important suggestion. If you travel to other countries, especially to a country that is very different from your own, you should keeping this saying in mind. For example, Japan has unique customs that is not found in any other country. If you traveled to Japan, you should find out about Japanese customs, taboos, and people beforehand.

ACTIVITY 2 Verb Forms

Read this paragraph carefully. Then write the correct form of the verbs in parentheses.

2 One custom is that you should (take) ________________ off your shoes before (enter) ________________ someone's house. In Japan, the floor must always be kept clean because usually people (sit) ________________, eat a meal, or even (sleep) ________________ on the floor. Another custom

is giving gifts. The Japanese often (give) ______________ a small gift to people who have (do) ______________ favors for them. Usually this token of gratitude (give) ______________ in July and December to keep harmonious relations with the receiver. When you (give) ______________ someone such a gift, you should make some form of apology about it. For example, many Japanese will say, "This is just a small gift that I have for you." In addition, it is not polite to open a gift immediately. The receiver usually (wait) ______________ until the giver has left so the giver will not be embarrassed if the gift (turn) ______________ out to be defective or displeasing.

ACTIVITY 3 Connectors

Read the paragraph carefully. Then fill in the blanks with one of these connectors:

because in addition even if for example first but

3 ______________, it is important to know about Japanese taboos. All cultures have certain actions that are considered socially unacceptable. ______________ something is acceptable in one culture, it can easily be taboo in another culture. ______________, chopsticks are used in many cultures, ______________ there are two taboos about chopsticks etiquette in Japan. ______________, you should never stand the chopsticks upright in your bowl of rice. ______________ standing chopsticks upright is done at a funeral ceremony, this action is associated with death. Second, you must never pass food from one pair of chopsticks to another. Again, this is related to burial rites in Japan.

ACTIVITY 4 Articles

There are 14 blanks in this paragraph. Read the paragraph and write the articles *a, an,* or *the* to complete the sentences. Some blanks do not require articles.

4 Third, it is important to know that Japanese people have ______________ different cultural values. One of ______________ important differences in ______________ cultural values is ______________ Japanese desire to maintain ______________ harmony at all costs. People try to avoid causing any kind of dispute. If there is ______________ problem, both sides are expected to compromise in order to avoid an argument. People are expected to restrain their emotions and put ______________ goal of compromise above their individual wishes. Related to this is ______________ concept of patience. Japanese put ______________ great deal of

_______________ value on _______________ patience. Patience also contributes to maintaining _______________ good relations with _______________ everyone and avoiding _______________ disputes.

ACTIVITY 5 Prepositions

Read this paragraph and write the correct preposition in each blank. Choose from these prepositions: *into, in, to, about, with, of,* and *around*. You may use them more than once.

5 _______________ conclusion, if you want to get along well _______________ the Japanese and avoid uncomfortable situations when you go _______________ Japan, it is important to take _______________ account the features _______________ Japanese culture that have been discussed here. Although it may be hard to understand Japanese customs because they are different, knowing _______________ them can help you adjust to life in Japan. If you face an unfamiliar or difficult situation when you are _______________ Japan, you should do what the people _______________ you do. In other words, "When _______________ Japan, do as the Japanese do."

Before you complete Activities 6–12, read the whole essay. Then go back and complete each activity.

ACTIVITY 6 Verb Forms

Read this paragraph carefully. Then write the correct form of the verbs in parentheses.

Essay 3

Dangers of Corporal Punishment

1 What should parents do when their five-year-old child says a bad word even though the child knows it is wrong? What should a teacher (do) _______________ when a student in the second grade (call) _______________ the teacher a name? When my parents (be) _______________ children forty or fifty years ago, the answer to these questions was quite clear. The adult would spank the child immediately. Corporal punishment (be) _______________ quite common then. When I was a child, I (be) _______________ in a class in which the teacher got angry at a boy who kept (talk) _______________ after she told him to be quiet. The teacher then (shout) _______________ at the boy and, in

front of all of us, (slap) ________________ his face. My classmates and I were shocked. Even after twenty years, I still remember that incident quite clearly. If the teacher's purpose (be) ________________ to (teach) ________________ us to (be) ________________ quiet, she did not (succeed) ________________. However, if her purpose was to create an oppressive mood in the class, she succeeded. Because corporal punishment (be) ________________ an ineffective and cruel method of discipline, it should never be (use) ________________ under any circumstances.

ACTIVITY 7 Prepositions

Read this paragraph carefully. Write the correct preposition in each blank. Use these prepositions: *in, of,* and *for*.

2 Supporters ________________ corporal punishment claim that physical discipline is necessary ________________ developing a child's sense ________________ personal responsibility. Justice Lewis Powell, a former U.S. Supreme Court justice, has even said that paddling children who misbehave has been an acceptable method ________________ promoting good behavior and responsibility ________________ school children for a long time. Some people worry that stopping corporal punishment in schools could result ________________ a decline ________________ school achievement. However, just because a student stops misbehaving does not mean that he or she suddenly has a better sense ________________ personal responsibility or correct behavior.

ACTIVITY 8 Articles

Read the paragraph and write the articles *a, an,* or *the* to complete the sentences. Some blanks do not require articles.

3 Corporal punishment is ________________ ineffective way to punish ________________ child because it may stop a behavior for a while, but it will not necessarily have ________________ long-term effect. Thus, if an adult inflicts ________________ mild form of ________________ corporal punishment that hurts the child very little or not at all, it will not get rid of the bad behavior. Moreover, because corporal punishment works only temporarily, it will have to be repeated whenever the child misbehaves. It may then become ________________ standard response to any misbehavior. This can lead to ________________ frequent and more severe spanking, which may result in ________________ abuse.

ACTIVITY 9 Comma Splices

Read this paragraph carefully and find the two comma splices. Correct them in one of two ways: (1) change the comma to a period and make two sentences or (2) add a connector after the comma.

4 A negative effect of corporal punishment in school is that it makes some students feel aggressive toward parents, teachers, and fellow students. In my opinion, children regard corporal punishment as a form of teacher aggression that makes them feel helpless. Therefore, students may get frustrated if corporal punishment is used frequently. Furthermore, it increases disruptive behavior that can become more aggressive, this leads to school violence and bullying of fellow students. Supporters of corporal punishment believe that it is necessary to maintain a good learning environment, it is unfortunate that the opposite result often happens. The learning environment actually becomes less effective when there is aggressive behavior.

ACTIVITY 10 Verb Forms

Read the paragraph and decide whether the underlined verbs are correct. If not, draw a line through the verb and write the correct form above it.

5 Last, corporal punishment may <u>result</u> in antisocial behavior later in life because it teaches children that adults <u>condone</u> violence as a solution to problems. Children who are <u>spank</u> learn that it is acceptable for a stronger person <u>using</u> violence against a weaker person. The concept of "might makes right" is <u>forced</u> upon them at a very early age. Furthermore, this concept teaches a lesson not only to those who are spanked but also to those who <u>witness</u> it. Studies of prisoners and delinquents <u>shows</u> that nearly 100 percent of the violent inmates at San Quentin and 64 percent of juvenile delinquents <u>was</u> victims of seriously abusive punishment during childhood. If serious punishment <u>causes</u> antisocial behavior, perhaps even milder punishment also <u>contribute</u> to violence. Research at the University of New Hampshire <u>will find</u> that children who were spanked between the ages of three and five <u>showed</u> higher levels of antisocial behavior when they <u>were observed</u> just two and four years later. This behavior included higher levels of beating family members, hitting fellow students, and defying parents. It is ironic that the behaviors for which teachers <u>punishing</u> students often get worse as a result of the spanking.

ACTIVITY 11 Editing for Errors

There are seven errors in this paragraph. They are in word forms (two), articles (one), sentence fragments (one), verb tense (one), and subject-verb agreement (two). Mark these errors and write corrections.

6 For punishment to be effective, it must produce a great behavioral change, result in behavior that is permanent, and produce minimal side effects. However, none of these changes is a result of corporal punishment. Therefore, we should consider alternatives to corporal punishment. Because discipline is necessary to educate children. One of the alternatives are to emphasize students' positive behaviors. Some research shows that reward, praise, and self-esteem is the most powerful motivators for the learning. Other alternatives are to hold conferences with students to help them plan acceptable behave or to use school staff, such as psychologists and counselors. It is important to build better interpersonal relations between teachers and students. In addition to these alternatives, instruction that reaches all students, such as detention, in-school suspension, and Saturday school, is available to discipline and punishment unruly students, too. Alternatives to corporal punishment taught children to be self-disciplined rather than to be cooperative only because of fear.

ACTIVITY 12 Editing for Errors

There are seven errors in this paragraph. They are in word forms (one), articles (three), sentence fragments (one), comma splices (one), and subject-verb agreement (one). Mark these errors and write the corrections.

7 In the conclusion, teachers should not use corporal punishment because it is ineffective in disciplining students and may have long-term negative effects on students. Moreover, teachers should not forget that love and understanding must be part of any kind of discipline. Discipline and love is not opposites, punishment must involve letting the children know that what they do is wrong and why punishment is necessary. Teachers should not just beat student with the hopeful that he will understand. It is important to maintain discipline without inflicting physical pain on students. Therefore, teachers should use effective and more humane alternatives. In order to bring about permanent behavioral changes.

Before you complete Activities 13–18, read the whole essay. Then go back and complete each activity.

ACTIVITY 13 Articles

Read the paragraph and write the articles *a, an,* or *the* to complete the sentences. Some blanks do not require articles.

Essay 4

Washington and Lincoln

1 Perhaps no other names from ________________ American history are better known than the names of George Washington and Abraham Lincoln. Both of these presidents made valuable contributions to ________________ United States during their presidency. In fact, one could argue that ________________ America would not be ________________ same country that it is today if either of these two leaders had not been involved in ________________ American politics. However, it is interesting to note that although both leaders made ________________ significant contributions to ________________ country, they lived in ________________ quite different times and served in ________________ very different ways.

ACTIVITY 14 Verb Forms

Read this paragraph carefully. Then write the correct form of the verbs in parentheses.

2 Everyone (know) ________________ that George Washington was the first president of the United States. What most people do not (appreciate) ________________ (be) ________________ that Washington (be) ________________ a clever military leader. He served the country in the early days of the Revolution by (help) ________________ to change the colonial volunteers from ragged farmers into effective soldiers. Without Washington's bravery and military strategy, it is doubtful that the colonies could have (beat) ________________ the British. Thus, without Washington, the colonies might never even have (become) ________________ the United States of America.

ACTIVITY 15 Prepositions

Read this paragraph and write the correct preposition in each blank. Choose from these prepositions: *from, in, to, with, for, between,* and *of.* You may use them more than once.

3 Abraham Lincoln was the sixteenth president ________________ the United States. He was elected president ________________ 1860 during a controversial and heated period of American history. As more states applied ________________ membership in the growing country, the issue ________________ slavery kept surfacing. There was an unstable balance ________________ slave states and free states. Each time another state was added ________________ the Union, the balance of power shifted. Lincoln was ________________ a free state, and many ________________ the slave state leaders viewed Lincoln as an enemy of their cause ________________ expand slavery. ________________ the end, no compromise could be reached, and the slave states seceded ________________ the United States in order to form their own independent country. Hostilities grew, and ________________ 1861 the Civil War, or the War ________________ the States as it is sometimes called, broke out. During the next four years, the Civil War ravaged the country. By the end of the war in 1865, the American countryside was ________________ shambles, but the Union was once again intact. Through his military and political decisions, Lincoln is credited ________________ saving the country ________________ self-destruction.

ACTIVITY 16 Editing for Errors

There are eight errors in this paragraph. They are in word forms (one), articles (two), modals (one), verb tense (two), and subject-verb agreement (two). Mark these errors and write corrections.

4 Washington and Lincoln was similarly in several ways. Both men are U.S. presidents. Both men served the United States during extremely difficult times. For Washington, the question is whether the United States would be able to maintain its independence from Britain. The United States was certainly very fragile nation at that time. For Lincoln, the question were really not so different. Would the United States to be able to survive during what was one of darkest periods of American history?

ACTIVITY 17 Sentence Fragments

After you read this paragraph, find the three sentence fragments. Correct the fragments by (1) changing the punctuation and creating one complete sentence or (2) adding new words to make the fragment a complete sentence.

5 There were also several differences between Washington and Lincoln. Washington came from a wealthy aristocratic background. He had several years of schooling. Lincoln came from a poor background, and he had very little schooling. Another difference between the two involved their military roles. Washington was a general. He was a military leader. Became president. Lincoln never served in the military. He was a lawyer who early on became a politician. When he became president, he took on the role of commander in chief, as all U.S. presidents do. Despite his lack of military background or training. Lincoln made several strategic decisions that enabled the U.S. military leaders to win the Civil War. Finally, Washington served for two terms and therefore had eight years to accomplish his policies. Lincoln, on the other hand, was assassinated. While in office and was not able to finish some of the things that he wanted for the country.

ACTIVITY 18 Editing for Errors

There are seven errors in this paragraph. They are in articles (two), verb tense (one), inappropriate words (one), word forms (one), number (singular and plural) (one), and subject-verb agreement (one). Mark these errors and make corrections.

6 The names George Washington and Abraham Lincoln is known even to people who have never been to the United States. Both of these patriots gave large part of their lives to help America make what it is today though they served the country in very different ways in complete different time in the American history. Although they were gone, their legacies and contributions continue to have an impact on our lives.

Connectors

Using connectors will help your ideas flow. Remember that when connectors occur at the beginning of a sentence, they are often followed by a comma.

Purpose	Coordinating Conjunctions (connect independent clauses)	Subordinating Conjunctions (begin dependent clauses)	Transitions (usually precede independent clauses)
Examples			For example, To illustrate, Specifically, In particular,
Information	and		In addition, Moreover, Furthermore,
Comparison			Similarly, Likewise, In the same way,
Contrast	but	while, although	In contrast, However, On the other hand, Conversely, Instead,
Refutation			On the contrary,
Concession	yet	although though even though it may appear that	Nevertheless, Even so, Admittedly, Despite this,
Emphasis			In fact, Actually,
Clarification			In other words, In simpler words, More simply,
Reason/Cause	for	because since	
Result	so	so so that	As a result, As a consequence, Consequently, Therefore, Thus,
Time Relationships		after as soon as before when while until whenever as	Afterward, First, Second, Next, Then Finally, Subsequently, Meanwhile, In the meantime,
Condition		if even if unless provided that when	

Purpose	Coordinating Conjunctions (connect independent clauses)	Subordinating Conjunctions (begin dependent clauses)	Transitions (usually precede independent clauses)
Purpose		so that in order that	
Choice	or		
Conclusion			In conclusion, To summarize, As we have seen, In brief, In closing, To sum up, Finally,

Useful Vocabulary for Better Writing

Try these useful words and phrases as you write your essays. They can make your writing sound more academic, natural, and fluent.

Comparing

Words and Phrases	Examples
NOUN *is* COMPARATIVE ADJECTIVE *than* NOUN.	New York *is larger than* Rhode Island.
S + V + COMPARATIVE ADVERB *than* NOUN.	The cats ran *faster than* the dogs.
S + V. *In comparison*, S + V.	Canada has provinces. *In comparison*, Brazil has states.
Although NOUN *and* NOUN *are similar in* NOUN, …	*Although* France and Spain *are similar in* size, they are different in many ways.
Upon close inspection, S + V.	*Upon close inspection*, teachers in both schools discovered their students progressed *faster* when using games.
Compared to…	*Compared to* these roses, those roses last a long time.
NOUN *and* NOUN *are surprisingly similar.*	Brazil *and* the United States *are surprisingly similar.*
The same…	Brazil has states. *The same* can be said about Mexico.
Like NOUN, NOUN *also…*	*Like* Brazil, Mexico *also* has states.
Compared to…	*Compared to* U.S. history, Chinese history is complicated.
Both NOUN *and* NOUN…	*Both* dictatorships *and* oligarchies exemplify non-democratic ideologies.
Also, S + V. / *Likewise,* S + V.	The economies in South America seem to be thriving. *Likewise*, some Asian markets are doing very well these days.
Similarly, S + V. / *Similar to* S + V.	The economies in South America seem to be thriving. *Similarly,* some Asian markets are doing very well these days.

Contrasting

Words and Phrases	Examples
S + V. *In contrast,* S + V.	Algeria is a very large country. *In contrast,* the U.A.E. is very small.
Contrasted with / In contrast to NOUN	*In contrast to* soda, water is a better alternative.
Although / Even though / Though…	*Although* Spain and France are similar in size, they are different in many other ways.
Unlike NOUN, NOUN...	*Unlike* Spain, France borders eight countries.
However, S + V.	Canada has provinces. *However,* Brazil has states.
On the one hand, S + V. *On the other hand,* S + V.	*On the one hand,* Maggie loved to travel. *On the other hand,* she hated to be away from her home.
S + V, *yet* S + V.	People know that eating sweets is not good for their health, *yet* they continue to eat more sugar and fat than ever before.
NOUN *and* NOUN *are surprisingly different.*	Finland *and* Iceland *are surprisingly different.*

Telling a Story/Narrating

Words and Phrases	Examples
When I was NOUN / ADJ, *I would* VERB.	*When I was* a child, *I would* go fishing every weekend.
I had never felt so ADJ *in my life.*	*I had never felt so* anxious *in my life.*
I never would have thought that…	*I never would have thought that* I could win the competition.
Then the most amazing thing happened.	I thought my bag was gone forever. *Then the most amazing thing happened.*
Whenever I think back to that time, …	*Whenever I think back to my childhood,* I am moved by my grandparents' love for me.
I will never forget NOUN	*I will never forget* my wedding day.
I can still remember NOUN / *I will always remember* NOUN	*I can still remember* the day I started my first job.
NOUN *was the best / worst day of my life.*	The day I caught that fish *was the best day of my life.*
Every time S + V, S + V.	*Every time* I used that computer, I had a problem.
This was my first NOUN	*This was my first* time traveling alone.

Showing Cause and Effect

Words and Phrases	Examples
Because S + V / *Because of* S + V	*Because of* the traffic problems, it is easy to see why the city is building a new tunnel.
NOUN *can trigger* NOUN NOUN *can cause* NOUN	An earthquake *can trigger* tidal waves and *can cause* massive destruction.
Due to NOUN	*Due to* the economic sanctions, the unemployment rate skyrocketed.
On account of NOUN / *As a result of* NOUN / *Because of* NOUN	*On account of* the economic sanctions, the unemployment rate skyrocketed.
Therefore, NOUN / *As a result, NOUN / For this reason,* NOUN / *Consequently,* NOUN	Markets fell. *Therefore,* millions of people lost their life savings.
NOUN *will bring about* NOUN	The use of the Internet *will bring about a* change in education.
NOUN *has had a positive / negative effect on* NOUN	Computer technology *has had both positive and negative effects* on society.
The correlation… is clear / evident.	*The correlation* between junk food and obesity *is clear.*

Stating an Opinion

Words and Phrases	Examples
Without a doubt, doing NOUN *is* ADJECTIVE *idea / method / decision / way.*	*Without a doubt,* walking to work each day *is* an excellent *way* to lose weight.
Personally, I believe / think / feel / agree / disagree / suppose that NOUN	*Personally, I believe that* using electronic devices on a plane should be allowed.
Doing NOUN *should not be allowed.*	Texting in class *should not be allowed.*
In my opinion / view / experience, NOUN	*In my opinion,* talking on a cell phone in a movie theater is extremely rude.
For this reason, NOUN / *That is why I think* NOUN	*For this reason,* voters should not pass this law.

There are many benefits / advantages to NOUN.	*There are many benefits to* swimming every day.
There are many drawbacks / disadvantages to NOUN.	*There are many drawbacks to* eating meals at a restaurant.
I *am convinced that* S + V.	*I am convinced that* nuclear energy is safe and energy efficient.
NOUN *should be required / mandatory.*	Art education *should be required* of all high school students.
I prefer NOUN *to* NOUN.	*I prefer* rugby *to* football.
To me, banning / prohibiting NOUN *makes sense.*	*To me, banning* cell phones while driving *makes perfect sense.*
For all of these important reasons, S + V.	*For all of these important reasons,* cell phones in schools should be banned.
Based on NOUN, S + V.	*Based on* the facts presented, high-fat foods should be banned from the cafeteria.

Arguing and Persuading

Words and Phrases	Examples
It is important to remember S + V	*It is important to remember that* school uniforms would only be worn during school hours.
According to a recent survey, S + V	*According to a recent survey,* 85 percent of high school students felt they had too much homework.
Even more important, S + V	*Even more important,* statistics show the positive effects that school uniforms have on behavior.
Despite this, S + V	*Despite this,* many people remain opposed to school uniforms.
S *must / should / ought to*	Researchers *must* stop unethical animal testing.
For these reasons, S + V	*For these reasons*, public schools should require uniforms.
Obviously, S + V	*Obviously,* citizens will get used to this new law.
Without a doubt, S + V	*Without a doubt,* students ought to learn a foreign language.
I agree that S + V; *however,* S + V	*I agree that* a college degree is important; *however,* getting a practical technical license can also be very useful.

Giving a Counterargument

Words and Phrases	Examples
Proponents / Opponents may say S + V	*Opponents* of uniforms *may say* that students who wear uniforms cannot express their individuality.
On the surface this might seem logical / smart / correct; however, S + V	*On the surface this might seem logical; however,* it is not an affordable solution.
S + V; *however, this is not the case.*	The students could attend classes in the evening; *however, this is not the case.*
One could argue that S + V, *but* S + V	*One could argue that* working for a small company is very exciting, *but* it can also be more stressful than a job in a large company.
It would be wrong to say that S + V	*It would be wrong to say that* nuclear energy is 100 percent safe.
Some people believe that S + V	*Some people believe that* nuclear energy is the way of the future.

Upon further investigation, S + V	*Upon further investigation,* one begins to see problems with this line of thinking.
However, I cannot agree with this idea.	Some people think logging should be banned. *However, I cannot agree with this idea.*
Some people may say (one opinion), *but I* (opposite opinion.)	*Some people may say that* working from home is lonely, *but I* believe that working from home is easy, productive, and rewarding.
While NOUN *has its merits,* NOUN…	*While* working outside the home *has its merits*, working from home has many more benefits.
Although it is true that…, S + V	*Although it is true that* taking online classes can be convenient, it is difficult for many students to stay on task.

Reacting/Responding

Words and Phrases	Examples
TITLE *by* AUTHOR *is a / an …*	*Harry Potter and the Goblet of Fire by* J.K. Rowling *is an* entertaining book to read.
My first reaction to the prompt / news / article was / is NOUN	*My first reaction to the article was* fear.
When I read / look at / think about NOUN, *I was amazed / shocked / surprised …*	*When I read* the article, *I was surprised* to learn of his athletic ability.